D0288585

A Year in Nature
with Stan Tekiela

A NATURALIST'S NOTES ON THE SEASONS

by Stan Tekiela

Adventure Publications, Inc.
Cambridge, Minnesota

Dedication

This collection of columns is dedicated to the many readers who look forward to each new "Nature Smart" column. I hope you will revisit every column here with renewed interest and enthusiasm and with the same zeal that I have for nature.

Acknowledgments

I would like to acknowledge Mark A. Weber for taking a chance on me and asking me to write my very first column. Thanks!

I am also grateful to all the newspaper editors who believe that a column about nature is interesting and mainstream enough to publish in their papers. This book is for you. May your newspapers be strong and everlasting in a time when the electronic media is dominating the world.

Edited by Sandy Livoti
Cover and book design by Jonathan Norberg

Front and back cover photos by Stan Tekiela

All photos by Stan Tekiela except pg. 117 and season divider pages

Some photos were taken under controlled conditions.

Copyright 2011 by Stan Tekiela
Published by Adventure Publications, Inc.
820 Cleveland Street South
Cambridge, MN 55008
1-800-678-7006
www.adventurepublications.net

ISBN: 978-1-59193-322-9

Table of Contents

Winter

December

January

February

A Naturalist's Notes

Nearly 20 years and 500 columns ago, I was asked by a friendly weekly newspaper editor if I would be interested in writing a short column about nature for the 10 weeks of summer. Apparently, summer was a slow time of year in the newspaper business and they needed some filler. The editor had just interviewed me about a book I had recently written and had published, entitled *Nature Smart: A Family Guide to Nature*. He was doing a typical story about "local guy makes good on book writing," so it was convenient to ask if I would be interested in writing a nature column. I thought, sure. I could do it for the summer. Twenty years later my "Nature Smart" column is syndicated in many papers throughout the United States, and I've never missed a deadline.

It's a classic story. It seems like yesterday that I started the column. The next thing I know, 20 years slip by and I am looking around wondering what happened to the time. The funny thing is, when I first began the column the editor asked me if there would be enough topics in nature to last the 10 weeks. At the time I laughed and said, "Of course—it's nature. You can write about nature for the rest of your life and still not cover it all." Little did I know what lay before me.

My "Nature Smart" column has changed a bit over the years. It started out as a straightforward story (around 500–700 words) about some aspect of nature. A story about the White-tailed Jackrabbit is a good example. Later I started adding my own photographs of the species I was writing about. Adding my images was a huge success. Once a photo was added, I really started to hear back from the readers. It was as if the images turned a light on the subject.

Then I started writing about my travels and adventures in nature. Since I write field guides for a living, I needed to travel to many locations throughout our nation to study and photograph plants, animals and birds. Many times I would photograph some of the craziest critters, such as a grasshopper mouse, which stands on its hind legs and howls like a wolf. Or maybe I would photograph an endangered species, such as the California Condor, as it soared over the Grand Canyon. All of these trips made for good stories and wonderful adventures to write about. I received the most mail, email and phone calls from the readers about these stories— it seemed everyone liked what I wrote about traveling. Happily, many of these stories are included in these pages.

Nearly all the columns are seasonal. They follow what is going on in nature at that time of year. I live in Minnesota, so during winter, cold weather and snow play a big part in my stories. You will read about many cold and snowy adventures. Other topics of interest, such as the turning colors of leaves in autumn, make for good stories also. Many times I had no clue what to write until the last minute, when I sat down at the computer. I would rack my brain trying to think of some interesting topic and nothing seemed right. Eventually I would come up with something timely and unique.

I think I've been able to write this column for so long because I am passionate about nature. Nature truly lives inside of me. I feel it and live it. I love all aspects of nature, from the weather to the insects and from the mouse to the moose. It all fascinates me, and I am thrilled and honored to be able to share this kind of information and spread the word of conservation and preservation. I firmly believe that the best way to take care of our world is to be educated about it. An informed person makes the right choices and takes better care of nature. And because of this, I will continue to write and photograph for my column and my books for as long as someone is there to read them and benefit.

Enjoy the Columns!

spring

sandhill splendor

We wake predawn and gather our equipment in preparation for a morning with the Sandhill Cranes of Nebraska. I am in the company of 12 crane watchers from the Minneapolis-St. Paul area to witness the annual migratory phenomenon of the Sandhill Crane (*Grus canadensis*).

After parking, our group huddles and in hushed tones we talk about basic rules before walking a half mile, single file, to our wooden two-story blind on the Platte River. As we approach the blind, the sound of the cranes intensifies and our hearts begin to race with anticipation. We tiptoe into the blind and open the small viewing ports, which reveal the river and the cranes in front of us.

It is still very dark and we can see only vague shapes of the birds and the reflection of the morning sky in the shallow meandering river. Now we just have to wait for the sun to rise to reveal the majesty of the cranes before us.

The eastern sky glows in tones of orange and red as the sun comes up. It is cool, but comfortable, and the wind is nonexistent—a perfect morning on the Platte. An estimated 15,000–17,000 cranes are milling about in the water. Some are renewing their pair bonds with each other by dancing, while others are squabbling and fighting. Still others are preening their feathers in preparation of the day's feeding activities.

Our group is awestruck, and even though I have been coming here for at least 15 years, I am again awestruck. What we are witnessing is the annual migration of the Sandhill Crane—an elegant 4-foot-tall crane with a red cap and yellow eyes.

For the past 20,000 years, cranes have been coming to this stretch of the Platte River in central Nebraska. The slow-moving river spreads out across a wide, flat area, creating many large sandbars and the perfect habitat for roosting.

Cranes spend the winter in Texas, New Mexico, Arizona and northern Mexico. During mid to late February, they fly 600–1,000 miles in a one-day nonstop flight to a small stretch of 65–80 miles of the Platte River. This is a migratory bottleneck, concentrating about 600,000 cranes in one place at one time, representing about 90 percent of the world's Sandhill Cranes. From here they fly for several days to a week to reach their breeding grounds in Canada and Alaska.

Over a 6–8 week period each spring, the cranes forage in the surrounding agricultural fields to feed on spilled grains and corn. Groups ranging from 50 to several thousand birds gather in the stubble of cornfields. Some look for food, while others pair off and dance and display for each other. They spend the entire day moving from field to field, gathering strength in preparation for the long flight to their nesting grounds.

The annual migration of a half million Sandhill Cranes to the Platte River in Nebraska is one of North America's most amazing natural spectacles and one of the top 10 natural events in the world.

Each evening after a day of feeding, the cranes lift off the fields and fly in large groups back to the safety of the Platte River. Long lines of cranes fly like ribbons against the orange glow of the evening sky. Slowly and deliberately the cranes circle down and gently come to rest on the sandbars for another night on the Platte.

The sun is up now and some of the birds are taking flight in the early morning light. We have full view of the massive group of birds before us. When we scan with our binoculars and spotting scopes to our right, we see one solid mass of birds. It looks like a large gray mass consisting of thousands of crane heads. There are no spaces between the birds. It is an extraordinary sight.

Over the next hour the cranes turn to face into the slight breeze and file out of the river in groups of 20–50. Some fly right past our blind at eye level, giving us wonderful views of these majestic birds. They are constantly calling, and the sound of a group this size is impressive.

As the last of the cranes leave, our group exits the blind and gathers in the early morning light to talk over the experience. Most of us are speechless and still basking in the glow of the moment. Warm smiles seem to be the order of the morning. We have just witnessed one of North America's most ancient and spectacular natural phenomenon. I am sure it will last in our memories for the rest of our lives.

Birding South of the Border

It was about an hour past sunset and the evening sky was jet black and filled with a million stars. I leaned back in the seat of the small, refurbished wooden fishing boat and felt the cool night air wash over my face. As the boat motored along, my mind wandered back to all the amazing adventures that have transpired throughout the day and it brought a smile to my face. It would be another 30 minutes or so before we would arrive back at the dock, so I sat back and enjoyed the night sky and my thoughts.

The boat skimmed across the still waters of the narrow tea-stained river. The boat's captain navigates through narrow tunnels not much wider and taller than the boat. The tunnels are cut out of the Red Mangrove trees that line the riverbank. The arching branches and aerial roots of the mangrove form a thick dense stand, and without constant pruning the passageways would be grown over in no time. Only a tiny light attached to the bow of the boat and the steady hand of the captain guides us safely down the river and through the maze of tree roots, dogging crocodiles and night-herons that are hunting on the river.

I am on the Pacific Coast of central Mexico, about three hours north of Puerto Vallarta in the wonderful small fishing village of San

Blas. I have just finished another wonderful day of photographing the wide variety of bird species that call this amazing area of Mexico home.

I am here for 10 days and as I write this, I'm on day five. Each day is similar. Get up about an hour before sunrise and pack all the camera gear and food and water for the day. Head to the truck and drive down to the beach to photograph the amazing variety of seabirds, such as Magnificent Frigatebirds, or drive up high into the mountains to find and photograph rare and elusive birds such as the Kalama Pygmy-Owl or magpie-jays.

Today was a little different. At 3 p.m. I met with a local guide and captain of this marvelous boat. He is a pleasant, retirement-aged gentleman with a wide, toothless grin and a nodding head. His English is limited to the names of all the birds in the area. So all you have to do is say the name of the bird and he nods, smiles and off we go to find the bird. What an amazing guide.

This evening was so incredible that my head was spinning. We started out this boat trip with scenes of wonderful birds such as a Common Black-Hawk that tried to kill and eat a Black Vulture. If you have ever seen the size of a vulture, you know they are huge birds—so this black-hawk must have had a huge appetite and an even larger ego. Needless to say, he didn't manage to catch and kill the vulture, but I got some great images of this bird.

We slowly made our way down the river, with a new bird species around each bend. As the sun was setting, we found a colony of Boat-billed Herons. This crazy-looking bird has a bill as wide as a boat—well, not really, but it's very wide—and a loud, raspy call that is unforgettable. I got so many great images of this secretive bird that I was just thrilled. And the best was yet to come.

By the time we got to the turnaround point in the river, the sun had set and the stars were starting to shine. Our guide turned the boat around and we started heading back in the dark. Using a large battery-operated spotlight, he illuminated the narrow river. Slowly we made our way downriver until he suddenly called out, "Potoo!" There, perched on a dead branch, sitting bolt upright was one of the most amazing birds. These members of the nightjar family hunt at night, using their huge yellow eyes to gaze skyward and watch for flying insects. When they see an insect, they fly out and grab the bug before returning to their perch. What really amazed me was the size of these nocturnal birds—nearly the size of a large owl. Each time this bird took flight to snatch up a bug, I thought I was seeing an owl.

Earlier in the day when it was still light we found a Northern Potoo, which is a bird of the tropical lowlands, sitting on its daytime roost. It is a nocturnal bird that sleeps during the day. In order to avoid being eaten during the day by other birds and animals, it strikes a pose on a tree branch that mimics another branch, making it blend in so well you would swear it was part of the tree.

The guide held the spotlight on the bird, and I was able to get some wonderful images. While I was photographing the potoo, other nocturnal critters were rustling up some dinner. The spotlight also illuminated several fishing bats. These highly specialized bats have enlarged feet that enable them to snatch small fish off the surface of the river in the middle of the night. Will the wonders of coastal Mexico never cease?

My photographic adventures along the Pacific Coast continue with a wide variety of strange and wonderful birds. Each day is sunny and warm and filled with another grand adventure and discovery. Some days are spent along the coast photographing pelicans and gulls as they skim across the ocean's surface. Other days we drive up into the mountains and tropical forests for owls and songbirds.

One of the more spectacular coastal birds in this region is the Magnificent Frigatebird. If you have ever watched one of the TV specials about seabirds, you probably have seen this bird. It is huge, with nearly an 8-foot wingspan. The males are black with a large red throat sac, called a gular sac, that it can inflate like a balloon to impress the girls during courtship. They are very distinctive looking, with long narrow wings that angle backward at the wrist. Their tail is forked and up to 2 feet long, like the streamers on a ship's mast. The females have white chests and black heads. The young have white chests and heads.

Of all birds, the frigatebird has the longest wings relative to its body weight. It is truly a seabird, but it never lands or swims in the ocean. Instead, it takes off from land and goes out to sea, soaring high over the water's surface, looking for fish, jellyfish, crustaceans and more. When it spots something, it swoops down, using its long thin bill to snatch it from the ocean's surface.

In the ports along the coast, fishermen bring in the catch of the day and the frigatebirds gather by the hundreds, looking for hand-outs. These huge birds circle overhead, waiting to swoop down and snatch up a scrap of discarded fish. Photographing them as they swirl overhead is

Many consider the frigatebird the pirate of the bird world, flying a black flag and wandering the oceans in search of food treasure. In fact, these birds are known to go to sea and continue flying for many days to weeks at a time without landing. They are helpless if they land on the water's surface, so they fly continually, sleeping and eating on the wing.

both fun and challenging. The local fishermen were accommodating and trying to talk to us as though we could understand. Once they saw that we were photographing birds, the fishermen sent two small children down to the water's edge to throw some fish scraps to bring in more birds. Then we really got some good images.

One day while driving along a tropical forest road high up in the mountains, a large rust-colored bird flew right in front of the windshield. I stopped the truck at a small opening in the thick forest and looked across the valley. There at the base of one of the many trees was a very large rusty bird with a very long tail and a large curved bill. My buddy Rick recognizes it immediately as a Squirrel Cuckoo.

Before I could ask the question, this bird starts to run directly up the trunk of the tree just like a squirrel. Once it reached the branches of the tree, it hopped from branch to branch with great speed, skill and agility. With its long tail and rusty red color, it appeared and acted just like a squirrel. Now I didn't even have to ask the question as to how it got its name. The bird briefly landed on a branch out in the open (which is unusual in dense tropical forests), and I was able to get just one image. Since my camera shoots 10 pictures per second, I would normally get dozens of images of a single species. But this bird was only interested in moving across the valley, and we never saw it again. It will be a bird that will stick in my memory for a long time to come.

I could go on and on about all the owls I photographed after dark, high up in the mountains, or the boat trips that we took out into the ocean to photograph nesting Blue-footed Boobies. Or how I was lying face down in piles of bird poop to get a decent image of nesting Blue-foots. But I guess that will have to be another story.

Sugar Mapling

Although it's still cold and wintry outside, there are signs of spring everywhere. Red-winged Blackbirds and American Robins have returned. Boxelder bugs are sunning themselves on the south sides of trees and buildings. Black-capped Chickadees are singing their springtime song. And another sure sign of spring is maple sap running within the maple trees.

There are more than 100 species of maples in the world. About two-thirds are found in Asia. Here in North America we have only 13 native maple species. All of our native maples share some common traits such as opposite pairs of leaves. Each leaf has 3–9 main veins radiating from a central base. All maples produce pairs (rarely in threes) of winged seeds, called samara, on a single stalk. These winged seeds are often called helicopters because of the way they rotate to the ground after falling from the tree. And all maple seeds are an important source of food for wildlife.

One of our most common maples is the Sugar Maple (*Acer saccharum*). It's a medium-sized tree averaging about 50–70 feet tall at maturity. It has a single large trunk with many ascending branches and a full round crown. Sugar Maples can live up to 200 years.

Like other maples, the Sugar Maple has oppositely attached leaves. Each leaf has five lobes (occasionally three) with pointed tips and a wavy leaf edge, which is called the margin. The leaves are yellowish green on top and paler below.

This tree is the well-known source for maple syrup and maple sugar. It takes approximately 40 gallons of sap to make a single gallon of maple syrup. In spring, any broken twig or branch will leak the watery sap. Many species of birds and mammals are attracted to the sap and drink from these natural taps.

Also called Hard Maple, the Sugar Maple has extremely hard wood that has been used to make furniture, flooring and cabinets for hundreds of years, and this continues today. A lesser-known maple is the Silver Maple (*A. saccharinum*). It grows in wet to moist soils, often in pure stands in the floodplains of large rivers and lakes. It is one of the first trees to send out flowers each spring. To the casual observer these are often confused with leaf buds. Leaf buds and their resulting leaves don't come out until after the tree is finished flowering later in spring.

Older tree bark is characteristic, with long strips that often peel and curl at the ends. The Silver Maple produces seeds every year, but it also produces extremely heavy crops every 2–3 years. It's often called Silver-leaf Maple, because the undersides of the leaves are silvery in appearance.

Silver Maples also produce a sap that can be collected and boiled down to make maple syrup. The yield is only slightly lower than from Sugar Maples, but just as tasty.

The sap flows in early spring when the nighttime temperatures drop below freezing and the daytime temps go above freezing. A typical tree can produce 5–50 gallons of sap each spring.

Fox Sighting

I had a wonderful opportunity to photograph a Red Fox and it reminded me of how much I admire this amazing animal. I was wrapping up four days of photographing owls in northern Minnesota when I saw this Red Fox trotting along the edge of a snow-covered field.

It was very late in the day, perhaps only 20 minutes before sunset. The evening light was golden, the kind of warm sunlight you often see in the best wildlife images. When the fox first noticed me, it hunkered down to hide among straw-colored grasses that were popping out of the snow—but it was too late. I had already leveled my camera at him and with a touch of a button, I brought him into sharp focus. It was now just a matter of time. For 10 minutes I didn't move or make a sound and neither did the fox. Sensing no danger, the fox slowly rose to its feet, its nose busily testing the wind to catch any scent of danger. Sensing none, he began to move about, hunting for mice under the snow. I began capturing images.

The Red Fox (*Vulpes vulpes*) thrives in every state and province of the United States and Canada. The population and distribution of the Red Fox increased dramatically after European settlement of North America, primarily because of the agricultural practices of cutting down trees to plant crops, but also because settlers killed off wolves and mountain lions, the chief predators of the fox.

Foxes are members of the canine family. Adults are 3 feet long, with the bushy, white-tipped tail fully one-third of the length. They weigh approximately 7–15 pounds—about the weight of an average house cat.

Even though the species is called Red Fox, it occurs in several color morphs—red to yellow, and black to silver or bluish gray. A fox's color doesn't change over its lifetime. It is born the color it will always be. No matter the color of the fur, one thing that remains the same is the white tip of the tail.

The Red Fox prefers a mixture of fields and woods, spending much of its time on the edge of the two habitats. It also likes suburban yards, woodlots, parks and golf courses.

A mated pair digs a den into the side of a hill or dirt pile. It's not uncommon for the parents to have second and third dens somewhere nearby where they can move their young if they are threatened. Breeding takes place in February and March. Litter size averages 3–5.

The young are called pups or kits and are weaned from mother's milk at one month. This is usually when you can see the pups playing around the den entrance. By the time the young are three months old they are on their own, often traveling up to 100 miles to establish their own territory. This is a very vulnerable time for young foxes. Many are hit by cars or killed by coyotes or wild dogs.

Scent Marks

When we talk about communication, cell phones and email are some of the modes that jump to mind. While we don't think about animal communication very much, their system is just as important and, in many cases, just as complicated as our means of communicating.

Nearly everyone is familiar with the ways birds communicate. Who hasn't listened to a bird singing and been amazed at the complexity and richness of that form of communication? In addition to songs, some birds use brightly colored or boldly patterned feathers to communicate. Think of these birds as flying billboards, announcing their messages to the bird world. Even in the mammalian world, the fur color and pattern of some animals speaks volumes. For example, the bold black and white pattern of the Striped Skunk is an obvious announcement that you shouldn't mess with this critter.

Animals also communicate by less obvious, but no less important, means. Most animals, if not all, use scent marking. It is a highly complex means of communication that is rarely detected by the average person.

Scent marking can communicate many different messages such as social status, sexual readiness or availability, boundaries of a territory, dominance, intimidation, orientation, an individual's identity and much more. While animal biologists don't understand much about this way of communicating, researchers are learning more about the chemical communication.

In addition to the standard base of knowledge of how scent marks are used, several new theories have emerged on the role of scent marks. One new theory is orientation. The orientation theory suggests that scent marks are used as a road map or compass for navigation within a territory. These scent marks would prevent the resident from becoming lost or crossing into another's territory, resulting in unnecessary fights.

Intimidation is a new hypothesis that suggests that in the absence of the resident animal, the scent mark conveys to an intruder the potential of being attacked if an encounter should occur.

Individual awareness is also a new theory that suggests that some mammals may scent mark within their own territory to demonstrate some self-awareness. Basically they are acknowledging their own existence.

Interspecies communication is a new thought suggesting that scent marking sends a message to disperse competing animals away from an area to prevent overutilization of the resources and overcrowding by similar species such as coyote and wolf.

Scent marking is usually accomplished with different substances such as urine, feces, and liquids secreted from scent glands. These different substances can be used alone or in conjunction. The response invoked by these scent marks is not scripted. In other words, the response by the receiving animal is not a preprogrammed behavior to the detection of a specific scent. The interpretation of the scent mark is based on past experiences, context, location, and even when the mark was placed.

Using urine or feces to scent mark is by far the most common form of communication as opposed to scent gland deposits. Placement of urine and feces is usually along major pathways or on prominent rocks, stumps or fence posts, and shouldn't be confused with an animal's need to empty its bladder or defecate.

Scent glands are found in numerous locations on the body, often near the eyes, on the feet, on the chest or near the base of the tail. Some glands are species-specific, while others are found across the species. Most of these glands secrete a small amount of oily liquid or a white paste material. The oily liquids are highly odiferous and tend to evaporate quickly. The liquids last only about 24 hours. The paste lasts for several weeks, but is much less smelly.

There is no doubt that scent marks are a very complex way of communication in the animal world. Now aren't you glad you have email and a cell phone instead of having to scent mark your messages?

Frog Chorale

For me, spring is frog time. It's a time when shallow, grassy depressions fill with snowmelt and April showers to create the perfect conditions for one of my favorite frogs, the Western Chorus Frog (*Pseudacris triseriata*).

To breed, Western Chorus Frogs require temporary wetlands or shallow ponds without fish. Hundreds of male chorus frogs pack into small wetland depressions and sing their hearts out to attract a mate. Like a well-rehearsed choir, the males sing an ascending, trill-like "b-r-e-e-e," lasting only 1–2 seconds. The call is similar to the sound made when running your thumb down the teeth of a stiff comb. The volume of all these

APRIL

male frogs singing together is often deafening. The large congregation of singers is how they got their name.

Since most frogs are small and live in inaccessible watery places, knowing what they sound like is the easiest way to identify all frogs.

The chorus frog is small in comparison to the better-known leopard frog. The Western Chorus Frog measures ¾-1¼ inches from the tip of its nose to the end of its torso. Females are larger than males. Both males and females have three dark stripes running the length of their bodies, called longitudinal stripes, and tan bellies with no markings. If you happen to see one of these tiny frogs, you can usually identify it by the dark stripe that runs through the eyes and the pronounced white line that extends along the upper lip.

Not only does their size vary—so does the color. While light brown is the most common color, they can be shades of green and red. The brown phase is predominant in warmer prairie areas, while the reddish and greenish morphs are found in forested, cooler regions.

Western Chorus Frogs feed on small prey items, such as aquatic insects, but they will take just about any other small terrestrial (land) insect they can catch such as ants and spiders.

After breeding, the female attaches masses of eggs (25–75) to sub-merged vegetation. An individual female can lay several hundred eggs per season. The eggs hatch within 12–16 days, depending on the temperature of the water. The warmer the water, the faster the development. After hatching, the tadpoles transform into adult frogs in 8–10 weeks.

The Western Chorus Frog is among the first frogs to emerge each spring. How frogs survive winter in northern tier states is nothing short of a miracle. Most people think that frogs overwinter by burying them-selves in the mud at the bottom of lakes and ponds. Research is now showing that this is not true for many frogs. Chorus frogs overwinter on land underneath rocks and logs near the ponds they call home. Since they don't dig down below the frost line, these tiny amphibians will freeze—something that until recently was thought to be impossible.

When they begin to freeze, the overwintering frogs greatly increase the level of glucose and other anti-freezing chemicals, such as urea, in their cells. While this lowers the temperature at which the cells will freeze, it doesn't stop the cells from freezing. More importantly, the cells containing the compounds don't shrink and the liquid doesn't form pointed ice crystals (as water would), thus allowing for freezing to occur, but without damage to the cell wall. In spring the process is reversed, and the frogs warm up and wake up. Sounds like something out of a sci-fi movie.

Ephemeral Wildflowers

There are many aspects of nature that might remind a person of the changing season from winter to spring. Thick sheets of ice melting from winter-chilled lakes, the return of migratory birds, the fanciful flight of Mourning Cloak Butterflies, or even the whine and sting of the year's first mosquito. But for me, spring is trumpeted by the ephemeral wildflowers.

Spring ephemeral wildflowers are a special group of woodland flowers. Often the average nature watcher might mistakenly believe that the first wildflowers of spring don't emerge from the frozen ground until May or June. Not so with the group of wildflowers classified as spring ephemeral. Ephemeral flowers are so named because they appear aboveground in early spring—they flower and fruit and then die back into the ground, all within a short two-month period, long before the trees have a chance to unfurl their leaves.

Ephemeral wildflowers, such as Bloodroot, Cut-leaved Toothwort, trout lilies and trilliums, emerge in April and are all gone by May or June.

They constitute one of the largest groups of wildflowers. By the time the warm winds of summer begin to blow, these flowers are long gone, often unnoticed by the casual nature explorer.

These remarkable wildflowers have adapted to the rhythm of the trees under which they dwell—a rhythm tied to soil moisture, soil nutrients and available sunlight, not to mention a very important relationship to ants.

Essentially a spring ephemeral wildflower appears early each spring, before the leafing out of the deciduous trees overhead, when full sunlight streams uninhibited to the forest floor. Sunlight is one of the keys to the ephemeral wildflower. If the flowers were to wait until the weather warmed up, the leaves of the trees would enclose the canopy of the forest and cut off any sunlight.

In addition to the sunlight factor, this is the time of year when soil moisture is at its highest because the trees aren't actively soaking up all the available moisture.

Soil nutrients are also at the highest levels at this time of year. A considerable amount of decay from the previous year's leaves provides a bumper crop of nutrients in the soil. The spring ephemeral wildflowers have first crack at this abundant food supply.

How do these wildflowers unfurl their leaves without any damage from unpredictable temperature extremes? The answer lies in the moist earth that buffers the extremes of the day and night temperatures. Plants can leaf out nearer the ground sooner than they can 30–50 feet above the ground. Supporting this idea is the fact that the earliest flowering ephemerals are shorter than the flowers that come later in the season.

In some cases, the earliest spring wildflowers, such as Bloodroot, are not only close to the ground, but they have leaves that envelop the main flower stem to trap warm air. Another successful way to trap warm air is with a dense covering of hairs, as seen in the Pasqueflower. This early prairie bloomer is so heavily covered with tiny hairs that it looks like it's wearing a fur coat.

Another reason to get an early start each spring is the availability of ants. Many of the spring ephemeral wildflowers have fruit (seeds) that are ant-dispersed. The seeds have adapted to attract ants, which carry the seeds to new places—even planting them in the ground to ensure future growth. Some seeds have a special oil that is especially attractive to ants, thus ensuring the ants will carry off the seeds.

Palm Paradise

This comes from the sunny and warm shores of Sanibel Island, Florida. It is a sun-soaked tropical paradise complete with tall, waving palm trees. But there are more than just palm trees in Florida. All things considered, the trees in Florida are an intriguing mix of eastern deciduous forest trees, such as maples, oaks and elms, which are found all across the eastern United States. But Florida also has tropical and subtropical trees, along with palms found nowhere else in the country. An interesting mix of trees indeed.

Palm trees have long been associated with Florida's beaches. It's not hard to envision swaying palm trees on a sandy beach or sunny boulevard. But has Florida always been one of the palm capitals of North America? The answer is yes and no.

Worldwide there are as many as 3,000 species of palm trees, with only a handful that are native to the United States, and most are restricted to the warmer regions of southern Florida and California.

There are only eight species of palms native to Florida, along with another three species (11 total) that have escaped cultivation and are now naturalized in the state. ("Naturalized" means the plant is now surviving and reproducing on its own in the wild without the aid of people.) All of these palm species

The trunks of palms are remarkably flexible—so much so that palms are often the only trees left standing after a hurricane.

are found in the southern half of the state, where freezing temperatures are not as much a threat.

It should be noted that there are about 25 species of palms that
are grown and sold in nurseries for commercial use in Florida. Most
of these cultivated species come from all across the tropical parts of
the world such as Cuba.

Back in 1953, the Florida legislature voted to designate the Sabal
Palm (*Sabal palmetto*) as the official state tree. The Sabal Palm can be
found just about everywhere in the southern half of the state.

Palms are very unique trees. They are considered more evolu-
tionarily advanced than pines and other evergreen trees, and they
exhibit a markedly different appearance than other deciduous trees.
Let's take a look at some of those differences.

The trunk of a palm tree is not divided into bark and wood like
other trees. Instead, palms have only an outer shell and an inner
cylinder, both of which consist of living tissue. In other trees, only
the thin lining just under the bark is living—the "wood" center is
dead. Also, the palm trunk grows from the center out, increasing the
girth of the tree without shedding the outer layer like other trees.

Another major difference between palms and other trees is the
unbranching trunk of the palm. Palm trees grow upward from a single
terminal bud, with a collection of leaves at the crown or top of the
tree. As the tree grows, new leaves erupting from the top center of the
tree replace the lowest leaves. The older lower leaves will dry and turn
brown before falling off. Some species of palms retain their old brown
leaves, giving the tree the appearance of wearing a brown grass skirt.

All palm trees can be divided into two major groups based on the
type of leaf. The first group has palmate or fan-shaped leaves. These
leaves are characterized by a leaf structure in which all of the leaf seg-
ments arise from a single point in the center of the leaf. This is similar
to the fingers on your hand, all of which originate from a single
point—your palm. The second group has pinnate leaves. These are
characterized by a row of narrow leaflets (smaller leaves) arising from

each side of the central stalk of a leaf, similar in design to a feather.

So there you have it—the palms of Florida in a coconut shell, if you will. The next time you visit the wonderful state of Florida, be sure to take a moment and admire the palms.

Spring Rituals

Spring—the time of year filled with ancient rituals that ensure the survival of the natural world. Each spring, birds and animals strut, sing, show off, chase, cajole or do whatever it takes to find a mate, with the sole objective of reproducing. The huge diversity of bird and animal species has led to a wide variety of ways in which the males prove to the females that they will be good fathers and worthy mates.

All of these spring rituals are triggered by the amount of available daylight. As the world tilts on its axis and the sun slowly gets higher in the sky, we gain more daylight. In fact, since the winter solstice in December (the shortest day of sunlight), we have gained over five hours of daylight.

The amount of daylight is called the photoperiod. The photoperiod triggers a hormone that activates the mating response in birds and animals. Mammals perceive the photoperiod through the eyes, where it passes into the brain. We humans feel different at this time of year because of the increased photoperiod entering our eyes. Birds, on the other hand, perceive the photoperiod directly into their brains through their skulls—a direct signal to the brain from the outside world, if you will.

In birds and animals, once the brain is informed of the photoperiod, it triggers the release of a hormone, which flows though the body and awakens the reproductive organs that have been dormant for most of the year. Unlike people, most birds and animals can mate only during this brief period of time each spring.

Once the reproductive organs are up and running, the mating rituals begin. In the bird world, the males are all dressed up to impress. The males of many bird species have brightly colored feathers that are designed to do one thing—communicate to females that he is healthy, strong and has abundant food in his territory.

In addition, the males enhance their bright feathers with melodic songs. Bird songs are as ancient as the species singing. Many songbirds have been around for hundreds of thousands of years. Songbirds are a specialized group of birds with wonderful complex songs that usually only the male sings. A few species, such as the Northern Cardinal, break the rules and both the male and female sing.

Birds that aren't songbirds, such as the Wild Turkey, don't sing at all. A male Wild Turkey relies on visual displays to show that he is healthy and worthy for mating. He will fan out his tail feathers, droop his wings so the wing tips drag on the ground and puff up his iridescent body feathers to impress the gals. He even flaunts the large patches of exposed skin on his head that change color from red to blue and white.

A male turkey will repeat a hissing and popping noise as he maneuvers in front of the females in his group to give them a good look at his magnificence. Only when the females are ready to nest will they pay him any attention and allow mating. The actual mating is brief, but the courtship goes on for weeks. While the male waits for a female's readiness, he will strut around and around so she won't forget that he is ready.

I look forward to seeing and photographing strutting male turkeys each spring. In my mind, their courtship is an ancient ritual that indicates spring. I get a sense of security and permanence, that all is right in nature when I see this primordial dance.

For you, the rituals of spring may be the singing of a male robin, Eastern Gray Squirrels mate-chasing in your backyard or cottontails bounding across your lawn and high-jumping into the air. No matter the form or fashion, spring rituals are important to a healthy environment. They ensure that the birds and animals will be around for many more generations—but only when the sun climbs high into the spring sky.

Timberdoodle Dancing

Dust billows up from behind my truck as I drive down the dirt road to my favorite location to see and photograph a strange little bird known as the Timberdoodle. Stopping on the side of the road, I step from my truck into a picture-perfect late evening. The sun has just set, but the western sky still glows bright orange and the sky is crystal clear. I love evenings like this.

Quickly I set up my tripod, camera, and most important, my flash. I grab my flashlight and walk toward a wet field with small trees on the edge of a large stand of woods. As I walk, I flash back nearly 30 years. I was a young naturalist, wide-eyed and eager to see all that the natural world had to offer. I am walking into the same field, this time with the best naturalist I have ever known at my side. She is showing me the display flight of the Timberdoodle. "What the heck is a Timberdoodle?" I ask her. She responds with the bird's real name, "American Woodcock." "Oh," I said, still not knowing what the heck she is talking about.

Shortly after sunset, we stand in the field and wait quietly. Countless Western Chorus Frogs in a nearby pond are filling the night with their loud mating calls. Then a loud noise breaks from the grass in front of us. It sounds like an electric buzzer. It's the call of the American Woodcock. Every few seconds it gives another call—"peent." Then suddenly it flies from the grass into the fading evening light. It flies up to a height of a couple hundred feet, and then starts to fly in a tight circle directly over our heads. I remember standing there, looking up and watching the display with my mouth open in utter wonderment.

I can hear twittering and whistling noises coming from the woodcock above my head. It flies around and around several times before suddenly it drops from the sky like a rock, landing back where it left the ground, and then it starts to call again—"peent." That was my first experience with the mating display flight of the American Woodcock. It is something I will never forget.

Flash forward to the present, and I am walking with my camera into the field in the fading evening light. I have the same experience of flashing back and remembering my first experience each time I come to see the woodcock display flight.

The American Woodcock (*Scolopax minor*) is a plump, short-legged shorebird that isn't found at the shore. Its favorite places are damp or wet meadows. It has a large head, and an extremely long bill that it uses to probe deep into wet soils for insects and earthworms. It has huge eyes on either side of its head, giving it the ability to see in front and behind at the same time.

The males perform this elaborate evening courtship flight each spring to impress the girls. Presumably the females are nearby on the ground, listening for a male with loud calls and a good flight pattern. When a female sees a male that is to her liking, she will approach him on the ground. Together they will fly off a short distance to a location nearby and mate. Afterward the male returns to his dancing field, and she will head back into the woods to find a place to nest, which is usually at the base of a large tree.

Tonight I am here to photograph the male woodcock. I work my way into the field as quietly as possible and I wait. I am enjoying the end of the day and it's getting very dark. From just 50 feet away I hear the first call of the night. I work my way closer just as the male takes to the sky to perform his sky dance, just as he and many generations before him have done for countless years.

His flight is perfect, and he comes back down not 25 feet away from me and starts to call. I turn on my flashlight and spot him standing in the grass. Quickly I focus my camera and push the shutter release. The flash from my camera goes off and lights up the small woodland meadow. The male doesn't even blink an eye—he just goes on calling. I've got my shot.

Many years have passed since that first night and there have been very few springs when I haven't come to witness the woodcock display flight. Now I bring my wife and daughter to this place to see the magical sky dance of the woodcock. The field is the same, but it is filling in with trees. The chorus frogs are still calling from the small pond, the woodcocks are still dancing and displaying, and I am still here to see the night dance of the Timberdoodle.

Baby Animal Rescue

Spring brings us many gifts of nature—colorful flowers, pleasant smells, warm winds, and multitudes of baby birds and animals in all sorts of shapes and sizes. Each year, naturalists like myself and wildlife rehabilitators get hundreds of calls about "abandoned" young animals and birds, and I am sure this spring will be no different.

So let's take a look at some of the do's and don'ts for the next time you find a baby animal or bird in your yard. Your actions might make the difference between life and death.

Before you rush to "rescue" a bird or animal, the first thing to do is take a minute to think and ask—is this critter really orphaned? The vast majority of young animals, especially birds, that you might see are not orphaned. It could just be a young fledgling bird waiting for its parents to feed it or a baby animal that is already on its own and doesn't need its parents. The key here is to stand back and observe the critter, and allow enough time and space to let the parent come back.

Let's take a closer look at what to do if you find a baby bird. A baby bird that is lacking a complete coat of feathers is always better off with its parents, so the best thing is to find the nest from which it came and return the bird. Don't worry about the old tale of mother birds rejecting baby birds that have human scent on them. This is completely false. Birds have little, if any, ability to smell. Birds that have been out of the nest for a while may need some warming up. Before returning them to the nest, you can cup them in your hands to warm them.

If the nest has been knocked down, try putting the nest back in the tree. It doesn't have to be in the exact same place. Birds have great eyesight and will have no problems finding the new location. If the nest has been completely destroyed you can gather some dried grass to line a small, plastic margarine tub. Punch a few drainage holes in the bottom and attach it to the tree with a wire in approximately the old place. Replace the young and watch for the parents to return.

Just about any bird that is fully feathered doesn't need rescuing unless it is injured. Fully feathered birds are called fledglings. Take a good look at fledglings before deciding to rescue them. If they have feathers covering their entire body and are hopping around on the ground, leave them alone. Even if they can't fully fly, they can usually flap enough to reach the lower branches of a shrub or tree, hopefully out of the reach of any cat or dog.

Fledgling birds are still being fed by their parents. If you don't see the parents, back away and watch. Mom and Dad are probably out getting a bug or worm for Junior. If you're too close, the parents will stay out of sight, waiting for a safe time to approach their offspring.

Finding baby bunnies in your yard doesn't necessarily mean they are orphaned. Bunnies that are still in a nest are being cared for by their mother. If the bunny nest has been disturbed, you can replace the nesting material and snuggle the babies back into place. If the mother has been killed and the babies' eyes are still closed, you need to take the babies to a wildlife rehabilitator.

Fully furred, open-eyed baby bunnies that are running around by themselves will be just fine no matter how small they look to you. Baby bunnies leave the nest at a very young age and are capable of taking care of themselves, even if they look too small to be on their own.

Baby squirrels are similar to baby bunnies. If a young squirrel falls from its nest, you should put the baby in a cloth-lined box and leave it at the base of the tree from which it fell. The mother will come down when it's safe and carry the baby back to the nest. If the nest has been destroyed, put all the babies in the box and wait for the mother to return. The mother will move the young one at a time to a new nest. All squirrels have multiple nests, and she will simply move the young. If the parent has been killed, bring the young squirrels to a wildlife rehabilitator.

This spring when you see a young bird, rabbit or squirrel alone or apparently helpless in your yard, stop and think before you jump to the rescue. If you need additional advice from a licensed wildlife rehabilitator, search online, look in your telephone book under "wildlife" or contact your local animal humane society or nature center.

Rabbits to Hares

There are rabbits—and then there are jackrabbits! And if you think there isn't much of a difference, you need to take a second look. I am not talking about the fluffy cottontail rabbit munching the tulips in your backyard. No, I'm talking about the monster of all rabbits, the White-tailed Jackrabbit (*Lepus townsendii*).

Despite its name, the White-tailed Jackrabbit is not a rabbit at all—in fact, it is actually a type of hare. Rabbits and hares are closely related and are members of the same family (Leporidae). Both rabbits and hares have long ears and large, powerful hind legs. Both have excellent hearing and outstanding eyesight.

Beyond these basic physical similarities, rabbits and hares are very different animals. The White-tailed Jackrabbit is significantly larger than the cottontail rabbit. Jacks stand up to 2 feet tall, including their enormous 8-inch-long ears, compared with the height of cottontails, at 12–16 inches. The average jackrabbit weighs about 7–10 pounds, while the smaller cottontail comes in at 2–4 pounds.

Now here is the major difference between hares and rabbits. After mating in February and March, mother jacks don't build a cozy nest chamber like the cottontails. Instead, they give birth to 3–4 young right on the ground. And unlike baby cottontails, baby jacks are born fully furred, with their eyes and ears open and with the ability to run within hours of birth. Compare that with cottontails, which are born blind, naked and helpless and don't leave the nest for several weeks, and you can start to see the big difference between these two species.

The jackrabbit's main line of defense is quick identification of danger and speed. Keen eyesight and outstanding hearing alert it to any danger. It can run up to 40 miles per hour for short bursts and leap 10–17 feet in a single bound. Not many predators can catch a jackrabbit at full speed.

Another major difference between a jackrabbit and a cottontail rabbit is its pelage. "Pelage" is just a fancy word to describe its fur. Unlike cottontails, jackrabbits change color in winter to an all-white coat of fur. In summer, jacks return to their brown or tan coat. This seasonal change is great camouflage and helps to avoid detection by predators.

Female jackrabbits are slightly larger than the males. This is of special note because while it can be common in the bird world, it is very rare in mammals. Adult male jackrabbits are called bucks, while the adult females are called does.

Jackrabbits are strict herbivores, eating green grass and other plants during summer and dried grasses, twigs and berries during winter. Their digestive system is not very efficient. During winter, when their diet consists of marginally nutritious food items, such as twigs, jacks produce two different kinds of fecal pellets or droppings. The first type of fecal pellet is hard, dry and woody. These are passed normally. The second type of pellet is soft, moist and green. These special fecal pellets are reingested (eaten again) in a behavior called coprophagy. This unusual behavior allows the food to pass through the digestive system a second time to extract every bit of nutrition.

Some may think this behavior is gross and disgusting, but I find it amazingly efficient and brilliant. It is also why these critters continue to thrive, despite the fact that nearly every predator is out for them. For these reasons I find these animals endlessly fascinating, and I hope you do, too.

Morel Madness

If you are at all like me, you can't wait for the month of May. By far, it's a month that has much to offer a nature nut like myself. It's a fantastic time of birth and bloom. The woodlands are filled with an array of spring wildflowers such as hepatica, bloodroot, trout lily, spring beauty and one of my personal favorites, trillium.

While many migrating birds have already returned to the northern states by the beginning of May, there are many more to come. Migrating shorebirds and warblers fly back to their breeding grounds in May, and no backyard bird watcher can deny the splendor and excitement when the Baltimore Orioles and Ruby-throated Hummingbirds return to our yards and gardens during this wonderful month.

However, May can have its dark side—a deep, lurking illness that hides during the rest of the year and harbors a disease that can cause the most normal person to act strangely, with bizarre behaviors. There is no cure for this May malady. What is this plague in our woodlands?

MOREL MADNESS!

That's right—it's morel mushroom time again. Run for cover, lock the doors and bar the windows! If you feel a fever and an overwhelming desire to crash through the woods in search of this elusive fungus, then you can be certain that the morel madness bug has struck. The only cure for it is a couple days searching your local woodland for the spongy devil.

Depending on the expert you consult, there are up to 10 species of morels (*Morchella sp.*). Fortunately, all are edible. However, there are several inedible mushroom species that appear similar to the morel. So let's go over some general rules to keep you safe, should you succumb to morel fever.

Morels grow during a short window of time, usually for a couple weeks in May. Many mushroom hunters use the blooming of wildflowers as the signal that conditions are right for morels. It is said that when trilliums or lilac bushes are blooming, morels are up and ready to be plucked. That means right now!

Morels have hollow stems and caps. One of the safety checks is to cut your mushroom in half lengthwise to inspect the interior. A morel will be completely hollow inside, like a straw. If there is any cottony material within, your mushroom is not a morel.

The cap or top of a morel is sponge-like (some say it looks brain-like) and covered with pits and ridges. A morel cap is connected directly to the stem. This means the cap won't hang over the stem like it does on a typical mushroom.

Also, morels don't have the paper-thin structures (gills) hanging under the caps of typical button mushrooms. Furthermore, a morel is a fungus that breaks down dead plant material (saprophytic), so it always grows on the ground. Therefore, if you find a mushroom that looks like a morel growing on a log or stump, it's not a morel.

I have some advice for anyone who hasn't gone out morel hunting. Don't do it—because it will quickly take over your life! Once you start hunting for these elusive fungi, there's no turning back. First, you'll start to neglect your family. Then you'll be calling in sick just so you can hunt for morels. Before you know it, your life is ruined. There is no cure for morel madness, so do yourself a favor. Stay home and paint your house. You'll thank me in the end.

For me, it's too late. I will probably be unemployed by the end of the month. I hope . . .

Red Admiral Butterfly

Have you seen them? Have you noticed their patriotic red, white and blue (appearing black) colors fluttering in the wind? For the Red Admiral Butterfly, it's a banner spring, and it seems that just about anywhere you go or anywhere you look, you can find another one. In some years, thousands of Red Admirals have been reported during spring. Some people have been lucky enough to see hundreds at one time.

The Red Admiral Butterfly (*Vanessa atalanta*) is a medium-sized butterfly, approximately 2–3 inches wide. It's a member of the Brush-footed Butterfly family (Nymphalidae). Except for the Lycaenids group, the Brush-footed group is the largest and most diverse family of butterflies in the world. It is estimated that there are over 4,500 species worldwide, with more than 200 occurring in North America. It's a large and confusing group of butterflies.

Like other brush-footed butterflies, the Red Admiral's wings are cryptically colored below and red, white and dark blue (black) on top. When perching with its wings closed over its back, the butterfly is very well camouflaged, blending into the environment. However, when it rests with its wings open, you are in for a visual treat.

Red Admirals are in the brush-footed family because their forelegs are very small and covered with bristle-like hairs, which resemble a brush. All adult butterflies have three pairs of legs (total six), but the Red Admiral walks on only the middle and hind legs. Their short and fuzzy forelegs are less than half the size of their other legs, but they are still very important.

The Red Admiral is about a third smaller than the more common Monarch Butterfly.

The forelegs have important sensors to detect the plant on which the butterfly lands. The hind legs have sugar-sensing receptors to detect nectar, on which the butterfly feeds. The plant-sensing forelegs help the adult females determine the right plants for egg laying. This is important because the developing caterpillars will feed only on specific host plants.

The caterpillar (larva) of the Red Admiral is covered with branching spines and hairy ornaments called antlers. It is thought that the spines serve to deter predators. The average nature nut often easily spots the caterpillars because of these spines.

Red Admirals are strong and fast flyers. Which brings me back to why we see so many of these beautiful butterflies in a banner spring. In northern states, nearly all butterflies survive winter in the pupa stage. This is the resting stage between a caterpillar and an adult butterfly. However, the Red Admiral is different. It spends the winter in the adult butterfly stage in the warmer southern states, just out of the grips of winter.

Each spring, thousands of Red Admirals fly northward to recolonize in northern states. They are considered migratory insects. Some years just happen to be better than others, which is when more than the usual number of Red Admirals shows up.

So if you are outside, keep an eye out for these wonderful insects. They are true harbingers of spring.

Snake Attitudes

Few animals are feared or hated as much as snakes. I am not sure where this came from. Some say it stems from references in the Bible. Others say they are despised because they don't have any legs, but are still able to glide across the ground. Subconsciously, it might be the unblinking stare from the lack of eyelids that spooks many people.

Myself, I like snakes! Maybe just for all the reasons that other people dislike them. There are more than 2,600 snake species in the world. They are found on every continent except Antarctica. North America has 115 species of snakes.

All snakes share similar traits. In general, they have elongated scaly bodies with no legs, external ears or eyelids. All snakes are carnivorous (meat-eaters only) and they swallow their prey whole. Some species mature after only a few years, while others take up to five years. Either way, snakes continuously increase in length during their lives. However, the growth rate slows considerably after maturity.

Most snake species, such as the Bullsnake, lay eggs. Others, such as the Common Garter Snake, give birth to live young. Most snakes are active during the day, but a few are active at night.

The Bullsnake (*Pituophis catenifer*) is a long snake, up to 6 feet long. It is a nonvenomous species that constricts around its prey to kill it. The yellow head best identifies it, along with the black stripe running from the eyes to the corners of the mouth and the many prominent vertical lines on the upper lip. It's usually straw yellow in color, with many (39–53) black, brown or reddish blotches down the middle of the back. While yellow is the most common color, it can be very dark.

The Bullsnake is a snake of open country, preferring sandy soils where it can hunt for pocket gophers (the reason for its other common name, Gopher Snake). It overwinters in underground dens below the frost line with other snake species such as racers and rat snakes. Bullsnakes mate during May. In June or July, females lay 5–25 eggs in self-excavated nests. The eggs will take 55–100 days to hatch, depending on the temperature of the soil.

Bullsnakes are good for pest control. Their main diet consists of mice, voles, ground squirrels, pocket gophers, frogs, ground-nesting birds and eggs. Since they don't have any venom, they seize their prey with their mouths and coil their bodies around the prey several times, constricting until the prey is suffocated.

When frightened, a Bullsnake will make every effort to escape. However, if threatened, it will respond with impressive fierceness. Typically, it coils up and rapidly vibrates it tail, hissing loudly and striking repeatedly. If the tail is near dry leaves, the vibration often sounds like a rattlesnake. With its mouth open, the Bullsnake expels air in a loud hissing noise while striking in an attempt to bite. Usually at this point, any animal that has threatened the snake has decided to leave it alone. The name "Bullsnake" comes from the snake's "bullish" defensive behavior.

Very few animals prey on Bullsnakes. Only the largest of hawks would take a full-grown adult. By far, the most significant predators are vehicles, when the snakes are crossing roads. In captivity, Bullsnakes have lived up to 25 years. In the wild they live only about 10 years.

It's about time we change our attitudes about snakes. They are like the good kid on the block with a bad reputation.

Desert Adventures

I love the desert, especially at night. Don't get me wrong—I love the desert during the day also. There is just something very special about the desert when the dark sky is perforated with millions of twinkling stars. Most people believe the desert is devoid of any wildlife. Nothing could be further from the truth. I have traveled all over this country to study wildlife, and it's my opinion that the desert is full of wildlife.

Several times a year I make a trek to the Sonoran Desert in south-eastern Arizona. And this is where you can find me now, surrounded by a multitude of cacti, sand and a wide variety of birds, reptiles and bats. I am here to study and photograph many of these, but tonight I am on the prowl for one particular bird, the smallest owl in the world, the Elf Owl (*Micrathene whitneyi*). It lives in this area.

It's just minutes after sunset and we just drove several miles on a very rocky, rutted road that required our truck to have high ground clearance and four-wheel drive. With me are noted author and photographer Rick Bowers and photographer Jim Zipp. We have parked at the base of a small mountain, hoping the area we chose for tonight's adventure will hold some Elf Owls.

Once we are out of the truck, we set up our cameras and flashes along with special high-powered flashlights for an evening of desert exploring. We head out into the desert night. It's cool with a light breeze, requiring us to wear light jackets—perfect weather for this kind of work. Within a couple hundred yards we come across the first of several Western Screech-Owls. They are calling back and forth to each other. We approach slowly, guessing their location by listening in the dark. We switch on a flashlight and sure enough, one of the screech-owls is right before us.

The owl is not in a good position to photograph so we switch off the light and move on to find another. We don't go far before locating another screech-owl calling. Again we flip on the light, and there it is. This time he's in the open and we set up to photograph him. We are all excited at the prospects of photographing this owl, but this is not why we are here. After just a few minutes we move on.

We move away and start climbing the mountainside, picking a path with the least cacti. The mountainside is steep and rocky. Each step results in dislodging some rocks, sending them down the mountain and running the risk of losing our footing. This is not good when you consider that on my shoulder is over $15,000 worth of top-of-the-line camera equipment.

About 20 minutes later we arrive in the area where we want to be and start looking around. It isn't long before we hear a male Elf Owl calling. We stop and try to pinpoint where the sound is coming from, and slowly move in that direction. Sometimes owls call so softly they sound very far away when actually they're very close. Only experience can guide you when this happens.

After more searching we locate what we have come for—the Elf Owl. He is calling from a cavity in a tall saguaro cactus about 15 feet high. Since we are on such a steep mountainside, the height of the cavity is actually at eye level, making it perfect for photographing. While setting up, the owl suddenly jumps from the cavity and flies off into the desert night. It doesn't take long and we see him flutter back to the nest cavity.

As I mentioned before, Elf Owls are the smallest owl in the world. They stand just over 5 inches tall, which is about the average size of a sparrow. But what I found so amazing about the Elf Owl is the way it flies. While trying to land at the nest cavity, it will flutter its wings like a butterfly. In fact, each time it landed on a branch or at the cavity, it fluttered. Its broad round wings looked just like a moth or butterfly.

It wasn't long before we were getting some amazing images, and my cohorts and I were thrilled at the opportunity. After a round of high fives, we were struck with the reality that we still needed to climb down the mountainside and there were a million cacti between us and the truck. Working our way back down I unfortunately ran into several cacti, which impaled their thorns through my pants and deep into my lower left leg and ankle.

Having no time to stop, we kept going until reaching the truck. I was able to remove some of the larger, more obvious thorns but the rest would have to wait. It was slightly after midnight when I climbed into bed. Each time I rolled over I could feel more thorns, and I had to get up. Using my pliers I continued to remove each thorn that I could find, but I couldn't find them all.

Two days later I could still feel some thorns in my leg. Eventually I got them all removed, but I must admit the experience with the Elf Owl was well worth the time and blood.

Bird Eggs

Each spring millions of eggs are laid, incubated and hatched by the birds that share the world around us. But have you ever given any thought to how amazing the egg actually is? The egg is a reproductive marvel— strong, yet not too strong to imprison the young bird developing inside. The egg is also waterproof, yet it allows oxygen to flow freely through the shell so the baby bird doesn't suffocate.

The shape of most bird eggs, with their large bulbous end and opposing pointed end, allows a runaway egg to roll in circles and not straight away from a mother bird. If a mother bird arranges her eggs with the pointed ends together in a circle, she can sit on more eggs than if they were side by side. Some eggs are round. However, birds that lay round eggs tend to be cavity-nesting birds, such as Wood Ducks, whose eggs have no chance of rolling out of the nest. An egg's shape is also the secret to its incredible strength. After all, the egg needs to hold up the weight of an incubating mother or father.

With all of this strength on the outside, the contents of the egg tend to be rather fragile. Early in the developing stage, even a moderate jolt or shock to an egg can be fatal. Eggs that have dropped from a nest during this time won't develop. So if you have found eggs under a nest, there is very little chance of successfully incubating the eggs to maturity.

The color of an egg is another amazing feature. When birds first evolved 60 million years ago, their eggs were probably white. Natural selection favored the evolution of egg color as a way of camouflaging eggs against predators. Supporting this theory is the fact that most modern birds that lay white eggs are cavity nesters (owls, woodpeckers, kingfishers, etc.). Since their eggs are inside a protective cavity where it's usually dark, there is no reason to camouflage the eggs. In addition, birds of prey, such as Bald Eagles, which have few natural enemies and therefore have nothing to fear or hide, also produce white eggs. The same can be said for most hawks and owls.

Ground-nesting thrushes produce brown, gray or olive-colored eggs to blend into the natural environment. Killdeer, ground-nesting shorebirds, produce tan-colored eggs with brown splotches, rendering them nearly invisible among their rock-lined nests.

Birds that nest in trees often have eggs that look like bark, with dark blotches of brown to help hide the eggs from egg-hunting predators.

The Common Murre, a colony-nesting bird along the Pacific and Atlantic Coasts, lays the widest variety of colored eggs of any bird. Each mother will lay a slightly different colored egg. The reason for this wide assortment of colors is thought to be a clever way a mother murre can identify her eggs among the thousands of other eggs in the colony. This example is certainly the exception to the egg color rule.

Brown-headed Cowbird females don't build nests or incubate their own eggs. They lay their eggs in the nests of other bird species and rely on the host mothers to incubate and raise their young—usually to the exclusion of their natural babies. Cowbirds lay gray eggs with brown spots. Their eggs tend to be larger than the eggs of the host species and acquire more heat from the incubating parents, which causes them to hatch quicker. This gives cowbird babies a competitive edge over the host's babies.

All of this brings us to the inevitable question. Why is a robin's egg blue? The best I can come up with is, in nature not everything fits nicely into the rules we humans think are in play.

Bird's-eye View

I am often asked how birds find food. Or another great question is, if I put up a new bird feeder, how will the birds know it's there or where to find it? The answer is simple—eyesight.

Eyesight is very important to birds. In fact, that might be understating the role of vision in birds. It's downright critical for survival. It is thought that birds have the best vision among all animals. And not just some birds. Nearly all birds have excellent eyesight.

This excellent vision comes from large eyes. A bird's eyes are so large that in some species the weight of the eyes is equal to or more than the weight of the brain. In many species the eyes account for about 15 percent of the mass of the bird's entire head. Human eyes by comparison account for less than 2 percent of the head and weigh a fraction of the brain. The largest eyes of any land animal are those of the Ostrich, which are nearly 2 inches in diameter. All of this space allows for more photoreceptors called "rods" and "cones" in the back of the eye. The human eye contains about 10,000 cones per square millimeter, while many of our birds have up to 12 times this amount or 120,000 cones per square millimeter (650 million per square inch), which gives them the sharpest vision in the animal kingdom. The Golden Eagle, for example, exceeds the visual acuity of humans by 2–3 times, allowing them to see movement of small prey from more than a mile away.

All of these extra receptors in a bird's eye allow many species the ability to see in specific light frequencies, including ultraviolet, which humans cannot see. Humans have three types of cones, each sensitive to different wavelengths of light or colors—red, green or blue. This is called trichromatic color vision. Birds have an extra cone for quadchromatic color vision (some have five cone types) that allows them to see the ultraviolet light frequencies. In addition, bird eyes contain specialized oil droplets that act as filters, altering color sensitivity in the same manner as sunglasses. Human eyes don't have these oil droplets.

Seeing in ultraviolet light helps birds in all sorts of ways. Many birds have feathers that reflect ultraviolet light. It is thought that this is used to communicate a bird's species, gender or perhaps its social standing. Seeing in ultraviolet light allows some birds of prey to locate their food by looking for visual clues left behind, such as mouse urine, which reflects a bright yellow when seen in ultraviolet light. The bird just follows the trail of color to the mouse.

Most birds can see well in low-light conditions. We humans rely on photoreceptors called "rods" to help us see in low lighting. We have about 200,000 rods per square millimeter. Some birds, such as owls, have up to a million rods per square millimeter, allowing them much greater vision in the dark. Rods don't help to see colors, but allow for amazing black and white vision after dark.

Nearly all of the 10,000 species of birds in the world have, in addition to the familiar upper and lower eyelids, a third eyelid called a nictitating membrane. It moves from side to side across the eye at right angles to the regular eyelids. This third eyelid cleans the eye's surface and keeps it moist. In many aquatic birds, such as the Common Loon, the nictitating membrane has a special window-like area in the center that presumably lets the membrane act like swim goggles to improve underwater vision.

The act of focusing on an object is called accommodation. Muscles changing the curvature of the lens in the eyes help accomplish this. At the same time, muscles changing the size of the pupil regulate the amount of light entering the eye. In birds, both of these processes occur very quickly—much faster than in humans. This allows birds to quickly focus on objects near and far and to change from light to dark situations in the blink of an eye. A Peregrine Falcon diving (stooping), for example, can keep focus on its prey even while traveling up to 200 miles per hour, and a songbird can see well enough ahead to avoid hitting tree branches while flying through a forest with pockets of light and dark.

As you can see (pun intended), most bird species see in the full range of color, like humans, and much more. Birds see the world very differently than humans—not because of their excellent eyesight, but because of the placement of their eyes in their heads.

We humans have eyes positioned close together in the front of our heads. This gives us nearly equal fields of view with both eyes, allowing stereoscopic vision known as binocular vision. Many birds have eyes positioned on the sides of their heads, leaving them with unequal fields of view from both eyes. This is called monocular vision.

At first you may think that having monocular vision is inferior to binocular vision. For the human species that may be true, but if you are a small bird looking for tiny insects deep within cracks or crevices or watching out for aerial predators, such as hawks and falcons, it would be far superior to have eyes located on the sides of your head.

Monocular vision has many advantages because it results in a wide field of view, sometimes as much as 340 degrees, which can allow a bird to see in front and behind at the same time. This would be like having the proverbial "eyes in the back of your head." Very handy when fast-flying predators are in the neighborhood and they are looking for YOU!

Some birds do have binocular vision. Owls, for instance, have large eyes close together in the front of their heads. Both eyes see the same thing at the same time, giving them binocular vision. Consequently, they only have a field of view of up to 70 degrees, and it's all in front. These birds don't need to see behind them because they are the predators, not the prey, and generally don't have to worry about being someone's lunch.

In addition, snipe, woodcocks and other birds not only have eyes on the sides of their head, but their eyes are also near the top of their heads, giving them excellent vision above without having to move their heads to see what's overhead. Remaining still is an important aspect, since these birds rely on camouflage feathers to stay hidden from a predator's view. If they had to move their heads around to watch for predators, the head movement would give away their location to a sharp-eyed hawk or falcon. Their eye placement also helps them watch for predators while probing in the mud with their long bills during feeding.

Binocular vision is important not only for owls, but also for many of the fast-flying predators such as hawks and eagles. Binocular vision gives a bird good depth perception, thus determining distances and spatial relationships easily. This is very important when it comes to capturing prey while traveling at high rates of speed. For example, a Cooper's Hawk often ambushes small birds at a feeder by quickly darting out of the shadows of the woods. The hawk is traveling so fast that in an instant it needs to determine what bird it can catch without running into the bird feeder, your house or a tree branch.

Although monocular vision doesn't allow for instant depth perception, it doesn't mean birds with monocular vision can't judge distances very well. The head-bobbing and weaving movements of the Rock Pigeon, or even a barnyard chicken, allow the bird to get a series of different views or snapshots to help determine spatial relationships of objects on the ground. When the head moves rapidly forward, objects closer to the bird appear to move across the visual field faster than those at a distance, giving them clues to the object's three-dimensional position.

If you want to see monocular vision working, you only need to watch an American Robin hunting for worms in your lawn. The bird rapidly runs forward, stops and cocks it head to one side or the other. Many people mistakenly believe the bird is listening for worms when, in fact, it is looking with one eye. The robin often cocks its head back and forth to gain a perspective on its food before quickly grabbing the worm.

Summer

Rocky Mountain Wild

It's midday in the Colorado Rocky Mountains and the sunlight has become too strong to take any good-quality wildlife pictures, so I am resting in the shade of a large Quaking Aspen tree. Known around here just as aspens, these trees are about the only deciduous tree that can grow at such high elevations. Ponderosa Pines are the only other trees that grow on these mountain slopes. They have trunks in excess of 4 feet in diameter. The rusty red bark riddled with black fissures makes this pine tree a very nice addition to the landscape.

My career as a wildlife photographer and nature book author brings me to many beautiful places and the Rocky Mountains of Colorado are no exception. I'm here working on *Mammals of Colorado Field Guide* and also *Trees of Colorado Field Guide* for this state. So here I sit with snow-capped mountains surrounding me and not another person for miles.

Each morning I get up at 4 a.m. and drive about an hour to reach my mountain valley. I park in a dusty dirt parking lot and gather all my camera equipment, food, water and, in today's case, my laptop. I tighten my hiking books and start the slow hike up to a wonderful stand of aspen trees. Situated at around 8,500 feet in elevation, I spend my days in this small valley, searching out wildlife to photograph. Not a bad day at the office, I would say.

From where I sit there are two very small streams—each small enough to step across, but full, with enough clear cold water to make a wonderful trickling sound. Sometimes during the middle of the day I stop to remove my shoes and socks and soak my feet. I can't tolerate more than a couple minutes in the icy water, but it feels good anyway. The warm rays of the sun help to offset the cold mountain water.

Yesterday while in this exact spot a coyote walked right by me. The resident Yellow-bellied Marmot gave a loud warning whistle, but the coyote didn't pay him or me any mind. He seemed intent on getting down the valley to the open meadows below, which is where thousands of small tan-colored Wyoming Ground Squirrels live. I am sure he had squirrel on his mind as he trotted silently by.

For those of you who live in the eastern half of the country, the Yellow-bellied Marmot is very similar to the Woodchuck, also known as the Groundhog. Marmots are high-elevation animals that live in rock piles and eat grass—and apparently petroleum products. I stopped my truck on the road the other day to photograph something when a marmot ran up and instantly started chewing on my brand new tires. Needless to say I had some choice words for my furry little friend. I had to shag him away from my tires several times before I gave up and drove off. Chalk one up for the marmots.

Elk and Mule Deer are found all over these mountains. In the higher elevations, Bighorn Sheep scratch out a living. About 50 miles south of here, up near the 14,000-foot mark, the Mountain Goats, which are all white and very shaggy, graze on alpine plants. I spent the better part of one morning following a herd of 17 goats around in order to capture some images for the field guide. The air was so thin I was constantly fighting to catch my breath. Even though the temps were in the high 40s, the goats seemed to be a little hot.

Within 100 feet of where I am sitting, I have located the nests of the Northern Flicker (red-shafted variety), Pygmy Nuthatch, Williamson's Sapsucker, Western Bluebird, Hairy Woodpecker, Clark's Nutcracker, Common Raven, White-breasted Nuthatch, Violet-green Swallow, House Wren, Steller's Jay, and my favorite, the Western Tanager. I am stunned by the volume of nesting birds in this small grove of aspens.

Within a few hours the sun will be lower in the sky, the light much more pleasing and I will get back to photographing again. Until then I sit in the shade of an aspen tree in a narrow valley in the Rocky Mountains of Colorado and write.

Firefly Light

Summer and bugs are synonymous. You can't have one without the other. While mosquitoes, ticks and many other insects can be a nuisance, some insects are totally amazing. The firefly is one of those amazing insects. I mean, who hasn't enjoyed seeing, chasing or catching these luminous bugs on a warm summer evening?

Fireflies, also called lightning bugs, are neither flies nor bugs. In fact, they are a type of beetle. Beetles are in the Lampyridae family of insects. All have biting mouthparts and modified front wings that cover their membranous rear wings. In other words, they eat other insects and have a hard shell over the hind portion of their body and wings.

Fireflies glow at all stages of life, including egg, larva and adult. Thus, the ability to glow only as an adult is not a characteristic of this group of beetles. To confuse the situation even more, not all bioluminescent beetles are fireflies. But let's leave the finer distinctions of beetles to the entomologist—one who studies insects.

A firefly starts out as an egg, which is usually laid in rotting wood or leaf litter on the forest floor. After hatching, the larva feeds on other insects and occasionally snails. Then it pupates (transforms) for up to several weeks before emerging as the flying adult beetle.

Although fireflies are found around the world, they are most common in humid tropical areas. In North America, however, very few, if any, are found west of the Mississippi River.

There are many kinds of fireflies, and each has a special way of lighting up the night. Each species flashes its own coded signal. Some flash a single brief light, while others give a series of flashes. Some flash while perching in tall vegetation. Others flash during flight. The results of the flying flashes are like skywriting, with some species creating a J or U or other shape in the night sky.

Why would a tiny insect have such an elaborate bioluminescent body?

To attract a mate, of course! Typically, males fly around shortly after dark, flashing the specific pattern of their species. Females perched on vegetation watch for the male's flash. Studies show that females prefer males that flash longer and brighter. When a male catches the attention of a particular female, she responds with her own flash, and a short flash dialogue may ensue between the potential mates. Afterward, the male will seek out the female by following her flashing. Once he has located her, they will mate, and she will go off to lay eggs and start the cycle again.

Revisit your childhood by going out and enjoying the natural fireworks of the firefly.

Fireflies produce light as a result of a chemical reaction of luciferin (a substrate) combined with luciferase (an enzyme), along with adenosine triphosphate (a nucleotide, or high-energy molecule) combined with oxygen. Obviously, fireflies control the timing and length of their flash, but how they turn the light on and off is unknown. Many theories abound.

What is known is that the light produced by fireflies is very efficient, with very little heat given off and lost as wasted energy. Nearly 100 percent of the energy a firefly uses to produce light is given off as light. In comparison, an incandescent light bulb emits only 10 percent of its energy as light—90 percent is wasted as heat. So I'm sure we could learn a thing or two about energy efficiency from our little summer friend, the firefly.

Showy Lady's Slipper

Summer has landed squarely in our laps with all of its heat and gooey glory. Furry mammals and feathery birds are feeling a bit sluggish in the heat, and so am I. Just about the only thing in nature that thrives in the heat are insects and orchids.

One of the most spectacular orchids is the Showy Lady's Slipper (*Cypripedium reginae*). The Showy Lady's Slipper is a member of the Orchid family (Orchidaceae), the largest family of flowering plants, with over 20,000 species worldwide. Most orchids are found in the tropical regions of the world. They are typically perennial herbaceous plants with complicated and very unusual flowers that almost always occur on a single stalk.

The genus name *Cypripedium* comes from the Greek words *Cypris*, a reference to the god Venus at Cyprus, and *pedilon*, meaning "slipper," together referring to the flowers, which look like the slippers Venus wore. The species name *reginae*, Latin for "queen," was given because the plant is the largest and showiest of orchids.

Individual plants stand over 2 feet tall with large, alternately attached, lance-shaped leaves. Each leaf is deeply ribbed with parallel veins that run the entire leaf length and clasps the stem at the point of attachment. The leaves and stems are covered with long white hairs, which may cause a Poison Ivy-like skin reaction in some people upon contact.

The Showy Lady's Slipper has some of the largest blooms of all orchids, up to 2–3 inches tall. Each flower is bisexual, symmetrical and has three white, pointed, upper petal-like sepals and one large inflated lower petal.

Each inflated petal is white with a rosy red wash and a fuzzy pale yellow "throat." This complicated flower structure is no mistake. In fact, the flower is designed for specific types of small flying insects. To get to the nectar they must enter the flower, but once inside they are not able to back out. The semi-captive insect must pass through the length of the flower's labyrinth in order to inadvertently pick up a packet of pollen, which must be properly positioned on the insect for correct pollination of another flower to occur. Thus, very few flowers become pollinated—but when one is pollinated, it can produce up to 35,000 seeds!

After pollination, the flowers produce a pod with thousands of dust-like seeds that are carried away on the wind after the pod dries and opens. Each tiny seed requires an association with a specific fungus in the soil for it to germinate. Once germinated, it takes the plant about 15–20 years before it matures enough to produce flowers.

These orchids require a highly specialized habitat to grow. Not only do they need the fungus in the soil, they also require a lot of moisture and an acidic soil. For these reasons, nearly every attempt to transplant these plants and beat the odds fails. Attempts to transplant only results in killing a very old plant and removes its potential for reproduction in the wild. So please enjoy these plants with your eyes and nose and camera only.

Leaves of Three

If you like camping, hiking, biking or just about any other outdoor activity, it's time for you to learn a new word. Can you say "urushiol?" Pronounced "yoo-ROO-shee-awl," it is the name of the oil found in Poison Ivy.

Poison Ivy is one of those plants that grows well nearly anywhere. It enjoys direct sun, but will also grow in the shade. It likes dry soil, but also is found in moist areas. You can find it mostly along paths, at the edges of woodlands, fencerows and thickets—and if you're really unlucky, decorating the border of your backyard.

There is a lot of confusion about Poison Ivy, Poison Oak and Poison Sumac, the toxic trio. Let's start by clearing up a few misconceptions. Poison Ivy and Poison Sumac are most common in the eastern United States, while Poison Oak is more prevalent in the West. Poison Sumac, which is much more poisonous than Poison Ivy, grows deep within acid/tamarack bogs, making it nearly impossible to touch. So put fears of Poison Sumac out of your mind unless you are in the habit of wading through knee-deep sphagnum moss.

Poison Ivy, on the other hand, is extremely common. There are some places that are filled with the nasty devil. The best way to avoid contact with this scourge of the woods is to be able to correctly identify the plant and avoid it.

Poison Ivy is a low-growing plant or vine with a woody stalk that splits into three branches. Each branch usually has three pointed oval leaves that only somewhat resemble an ivy-shaped leaf.

Poison Ivy is a master of disguise. Its leaves are usually shiny, but can be dull. The edge of each leaf can be smooth or have

The urushiol oil in Poison Ivy can also lay in wait for you on garden tools, clothing and even on your pet for up to year. So let this be a warning to you about messing with Poison Ivy. If you think you have been exposed to this menace, the best treatment is water or rubbing alcohol, and lots of it. Scrub the affected area with an alcohol-water mixture and wash all clothing in hot soapy water.

large teeth. It grows on the ground, but also vines high into trees. About the only consistent characteristics are its woody stem, yellow-to-green flowers (which produce green-to-white berries after the plant is three years old) and a middle leaf stem, called a petiole, that is longer than the other two stems on either side. It is also one of the first plants to turn deep red each autumn. A good way to identify Poison Ivy and avoid it is to remember the old saying, "Leaves of three, leave them be."

Interestingly, it appears that only people have troubles with Poison Ivy. Animals, birds and other wild critters have no problems with the plant. Birds and bears eat the berries and deer eat the leaves without suffering adverse reactions. Many cases of Poison Ivy in humans are, in fact, transmitted from the family pets, such as dogs and cats, to their owners.

The only way to get Poison Ivy is to come in contact with our friend, urushiol. Urushiol oil is found in every part of the plant except the flowers. The oil, which causes the allergic reaction, has the consistency and color of 3-IN-ONE oil. Only if the plant is damaged in some fashion will the oil leak out. That is the point when the oil is transferred to you. When heated, urushiol splatters like butter. It will attach to smoke particles and can cause serious rashes to anyone downwind. Nationally, only

10 percent of the human population is truly immune to its ill effects. So if you are one of those who claim immunity to Poison Ivy, it may be that you have never come in contact with the plant.

There are hundreds of home remedies, most of which are ineffective. A minor rash of Poison Ivy can be handled at home, but your doctor should treat a serious case. It has been said that Poison Ivy left untreated will last about two weeks, while a case that is treated will last only 14 days. So make it your duty this season to be able to recognize this one amazing plant, and steer clear of this home wrecker of the woodland.

Wood Ticks

Just bring up the words "wood tick" and even the most ardent nature lover cringes and starts to get the heebie-geebies. Even as I write this, my skin is crawling.

As a naturalist, I try to look for the good in all aspects of nature. I've spent my career explaining the virtues of plants, such as Poison Ivy, and birds, such as the American Crow, to people who find them unfavorable. I try to convey something interesting that might spark a new way of looking at the "bad" plant or animal, something that might make you say, "Gee-whiz, that's interesting!" But I seem to be at a loss for words when it comes to the wood tick—but here goes anyway.

Ticks are members of the Mites and Ticks (Acari) order, which are closely related to spiders. There are over 1,000 named species of ticks worldwide. Some estimate there are up to a half million more tick species yet to be discovered. Now there's a comforting thought.

There are two types of ticks—hard-bodied and soft-bodied. Wood ticks are hard-bodied and so named because of the hard plate on top of their bodies. This is also why it's difficult to kill them simply by squeezing or crushing. Soft-bodied ticks lack the hard plate and have mouthparts under their heads unlike hard ticks, which have mouthparts in front of their heads.

Newly hatched young, called larvae, have only six legs. They are extremely tiny and obtain two more legs after the first molt, for a total of eight legs, like spiders. Just like the adults, the larvae also feed on blood, but they concentrate on small animals such as mice and voles. With each blood meal (total of 3–5), the larvae molt (shed their old skin) and grow larger. Once they reach adult size, they feed on larger mammals such as deer and people.

To find their hosts, ticks cling to the tips of plants and extend their forelegs to grab any passing mammal. They may remain perched on the end of a twig or blade of grass for weeks before a large mammal passes by within reach. Once they have landed on a potential host, they often climb to the highest point and search for a warm and protected spot such as behind the ears, nape of the neck or the collar. (Are you starting to itch now?) Once in position, they use their forward-facing mouthparts to pierce the skin and begin to feed on the blood. Once fully engorged, they drop off and molt and lay eggs.

Mature females mate, but don't lay eggs until they've had a blood meal, which could be months later. From the nutrients in the blood, the female will develop many eggs. Afterward she deposits them and dies. The eggs hatch into tiny six-legged larvae, and the cycle starts over again.

Most full-grown wood ticks are ⅛ inch long. Males and females are the same size, but you can tell them apart. Males are reddish brown with two white stripes running lengthwise down their bodies. Females are the same color, but have a single U-shaped mark. An easy way to differentiate the sexes is to remember that the males look like they are wearing suspenders, while the females look like they are wearing a necklace.

Wood ticks are sometimes called American Dog Tick. Because they feed directly on blood, they can transfer disease from one host to the next, including Rocky Mountain spotted fever, tularemia and tick paralysis.

If you find a tick attached to your body, you can carefully remove it with tweezers. Grasp it around the head as close to your skin as possible, and gently yet firmly pull it out. Home remedies, such as covering the tick with Vaseline or burning it off with a hot match, do not work. Save any ticks that were attached for prolonged periods of time for identification by an expert.

Of course, the best way to avoid getting a tick bite is to steer clear of ticks in the first place. Avoid walking in tall grass. Wear long sleeves and long pants. Tuck your pants into your socks so you can see the tick crawling up the outside of your pants, not inside. Apply insect repellent, such as products containing DEET (N,N-diethyl-meta-toluamide), to clothing. Naturally, consult your doctor before applying DEET to children. And always check yourself for ticks as soon as possible.

As for me, ticks don't bother me as much as those darn mosquitoes that drive me crazy.

Yellow Rail Birding

It is 11:30 p.m. and the moon hasn't come up yet. Above me are millions of stars shining brightly in the black night sky. Below me is ankle-deep water and a continuous waist-deep mat of reeds, sedges and grass for hundreds of acres in all directions. At times it seems there are as many lightning bugs as there are stars in the sky. Each step I take is fraught with peril. The spongy mat feels stable underfoot until my entire weight is applied and then it's back into ankle-deep water. Every now and then the bottom drops out and my foot plunges in deeper, bringing the water up to mid-thigh. The thick mat of vegetation grabs at my feet and ankles and tries to trip me with each step I take in the darkness.

It has taken the three of us nearly 30 minutes to "walk" only 300 yards and we are still not to our destination. A friend let me use a pair of chest waders that are too large and missing the suspenders. I have fashioned a bungee cord to hold up the rubberized boots and it is now cutting deeply into my shoulders. And as usual, I am carrying several thousand dollars of camera equipment that won't fare well if dropped in the water.

What I have come to see and photograph in this northern Minnesota location is one of the most secretive and elusive birds in North America—the Yellow Rail (*Coturnicops noveboracensis*). In the darkness I can hear the rhythmic tapping call of the bird just ahead of us. A few more steps and we should be there.

Slowly and quietly, or as quiet as one can be while walking in such conditions, we approach the sound. Deep within the thick vegetation the male Yellow Rail is giving its mating call. The sound is similar to the sound made by two small stones being tapped together in a very rapid and irregular pattern.

After what seemed like a very long time of trying to locate the bird in the dark, we decide that the bird must be directly in front of us—so we switch on the flashlight. Nothing! The sound is loud and strong, but we are unable to see the bird. We switch off the light and stand in the dark listening again to the rhythmic tapping. This goes on for the next hour. Switching on the light, scanning the area, and then switching it off again.

Our hopes of seeing and photographing this bird were fading when about 1 a.m. we switch on the light and there in the beam of our flashlight is a small brown bird about the size of a sparrow with a short, stout yellow bill. Its body is plump and round with a short pointed tail. It has long legs and large feet, but the thick grass has hidden this feature.

Rails are a type of marsh bird with short round wings and stubby tails. They have long legs and large feet to help them navigate in thick, watery habitat. Marsh birds are usually secretive and hard to see, but the Yellow Rail is especially secretive—and to make things even more difficult, it is also nocturnal. Yellow Rails are one of North America's most elusive and mysterious birds. There is no data on population, but estimates are around 10,000–20,000.

Very little is known about the Yellow Rail's biology, wintering grounds or other simple facts. What is known is they nest across northern Minnesota and North Dakota northward into southern Canada and they winter along the Gulf Coast and throughout Florida. They migrate by themselves at night. After mating, the female builds a nest in the reeds and grasses and lays 8–10 eggs. After hatching, the young leave the nest within 24–48 hours to forage and are caring for themselves by three weeks of age.

Standing in the beam of light, our bird has stopped calling and remains still. The flash from my camera lights up the immediate area like a lightning bolt. Again and again the flash goes off and the bird doesn't even react. Slowly it starts to preen its feathers and go about its nocturnal activities as if nothing has happened.

In hushed whispers we congratulate each other on this outstanding find and photographic opportunity. Just at that moment we realize we have a long and treacherous walk back to our cars. We turn in the darkness and start the long slow march back with very large grins on our faces.

Bracken Cave

I must have an affinity for anything that flies. Otherwise, what else would explain way I am standing in the middle of the hill country of Texas on a hot and steamy summer evening? It's almost 7 p.m., the temperature is still 101 degrees and the humidity is ridiculously high. Just standing here, the sweat is dripping down my back.

Even though you can cut the hot summer air with a knife, it hasn't rained in several months. Instead of a being surrounded by a lush green landscape, the hills, fields and roadsides are every shade of brown, indicating the drought. A very strange dichotomy indeed.

So what brings me to central Texas at this hot and uncomfortable time of year? Well, if you know me at all, you're probably guessing it's some kind of rare and interesting bird. Well, that's close, but it's not a bird that brings me to Texas. It is a mammal—the Brazilian Free-tailed Bat, also called the Mexican Free-tailed Bat.

I've come to Bracken Cave, a large 600-foot-long cave that is owned and protected by Bat Conservation International (BCI). It's a highly restricted cave and I'm here by private invite. For at least the last 10,000 years, this cave has been home to millions of bats each summer.

The entrance of the cave sits at the side of a large depression in the ground. Approaching the cave from the east, you can't help but smell the characteristic odor of an active bat cave. The pungent smell floats around on the warm summer's breeze as natural as a fence post lizard scrambles among rocks.

Other caves in Texas have large numbers of free-tailed bats, but not as many as Bracken Cave.

Moving around to the western side of the cave, a large eyebrow-shaped entrance comes into view. Even though it is not quite two hours before sunset, there are already thousands of bats swirling around at the cave entrance. Moving in perfect concert with each other, the bats fly in ever-expanding circles, with half of the circle inside the cave and the other half outside. Around and around they go. It's a very impressive sight and I am getting excited at the prospect of the event that is about to unfold before me.

As I set up my camera gear and flash, I can see the amount of swirling bats building at the cave entrance. The swirling mass of bats is bulging and now more than half of the flight circle is outside the cave. I can hear the flapping of all those wings. For some reason I expected more noise and more chaos, but it's very quiet and well organized.

Now the swirling mass of bats has moved completely out of the cave entrance and is gaining altitude. Like a spinning vortex, the massive group of thousands ascends, filling the evening sky. At this moment I can feel the wash of air produced from all the wings beating together. The first batch of bats in the vortex is now joined by many more thousands of bats exiting the cave. At the apex of the swirling mass, the bats stream off toward the horizon in a snaking column. The column is long and so thick it appears like a trail of smoke or a river of bats. At this moment it is a solid mass of bats emerging from the cave entrance, rising up 100 feet and trailing off and over the horizon.

There are so many bats emerging from this cave that the local Doppler radar clearly registers the mass. There are an estimated 20 million bats in this one cave. This is the largest gathering of a single mammal species on the face of the earth. All of these bats are pregnant females, each giving birth to a single pup. By end of summer, presuming all the females give birth and all the young live, there could be 40 million bats in the cave. However, many of the young don't survive so it is estimated that at least 30 million bats will leave the cave at summer's end to migrate south.

There are so many bats in the cave that the bats stream out of the entrance for hours on end all evening. Each mother bat needs to go out and feed to maintain its health and be able to nurse its baby. Each mother bat consumes up to half its own body weight in insects each night, for an estimated 200 tons of insects. Many of these insects are agricultural pests. It is estimated that the bats save local ranchers and farmers $1.75 million in pesticide use alone.

Upon returning to the cave, the bats are so tightly packed that the ceiling of the cave has over 200 individuals per square foot. The body heat from all of these bats raises the temperature in the cave from a natural 68 degrees to over 100 degrees.

Watching bats emerge from the cave this evening is an unforgettable experience. I travel the world to study, photograph and document natural history, and Bracken Cave is near the top of my list of truly wonderful places.

Nighthawks

The Bullbats of summer are back in town. Flying fast and loose through the evening sky, Bullbats are the bad boys of the night. This is not good news if you are a flying insect!

Never heard of a Bullbat? Well, how about a nighthawk? That's right, the Bullbat and Common Nighthawk (*Chordeiles minor*) are the same bird. While the name "Bullbat" sounds impressive, the bird is neither a bull nor a bat. That's the problem with common names. They can be misleading.

The same can be said for the name "Nighthawk." Although it's the more accepted common name, it is still a poor description of this bird. The "Night" reference works because the bird becomes most active during the evening, but "hawk" is way off. The nighthawk is not a hawk. For instance, it lacks the strong feet and talons of a hawk and also the sharp, curved, flesh-tearing bill of hawks. Well, I think you understand what I am trying to get at.

The Common Nighthawk is a large brown bird that you might have seen or heard near dusk on a warm summer's evening. It has long pointed wings and a slightly forked tail. Most people recognize the bold white bands or stripes across its wings and tail.

It is a very noisy bird, repeating a nasal "peenting" call during its very erratic flight pattern. It alternates slow, full wing beats with bursts of quick, shallow beats while it hunts for flying insects. In fact, this bird eats more flying insects than just about any bird.

The nighthawk is often seen in groups of up to 30 individuals flying above parking lots, suburban streets and yards. It is very common in the largest cities and can be more of a city bird than a country bird sometimes. The males can be distinguished from females by their white throat patch and white band across the tail compared with the tan throat patch of the females and lack of a tail band.

Nighthawks are ground nesters, finding flat, gravel-covered rooftops to be irresistible. The female does not build a nest, preferring to create a depression in the gravel to lay her eggs. The camouflage brown and white coloring of both the male and female makes them nearly invisible among the rocks while incubating.

If you spend any time watching these birds, you are bound to notice a very interesting behavior. The males perform a spectacular mating flight. It consists of flying straight up to a dizzying height, then turning and dropping in a steep diving flight that is terminated with a loud buzzing, and then a popping noise.

It was once thought that the white bands on the wings somehow caused this popping noise. Then for a while it was thought that the bird opening its oversized mouth to catch some air caused the noise. Neither of these is true. The noise is caused by air rushing over the stiff wing feathers. Why the male bird does steep diving is still a mystery. My guess is that it's to impress a possible mate. Either way, it is an impressive sight and sound. I encourage you to step outside this evening to witness these bad boys of summer.

Grasshopper Mouse Fun

I returned from eight days in one of my favorite places in the whole wide world—the Sonoran Desert in southeastern Arizona. Ya, I know what you're thinking. What the heck was I thinking, going to the desert in the middle of summer? Well, it's actually not as bad as you might think. I do this every year. In fact, it is by far the most wildlife-rich area I have ever seen, even in all the sun-baked heat.

First of all, it's the monsoon season in the desert. This means each afternoon in the peak of the oppressive heat, clouds build up and thunderstorms break out all over the place, which helps to cool things down. Although rain has been nearly nonexistent this year, the clouds did help to cool things even without the associated rain.

Before the days got too hot, I spent my early mornings photographing hummingbirds. There were up to eight species of hummers congregating at nectar feeders. I stopped in to see a friend who was keeping track of how many hummingbirds she was feeding every day during their migration. By measuring exactly how much nectar (sugar water) the hummers were consuming each day, she was able to calculate how many hummingbirds were visiting her feeders. On the day I visited, she had 1,416 hummers that drank 8.18 quarts of nectar in one day. That was the highest count of hummers during the fall migration that she had ever seen in her 10 years of monitoring. Her feeders were swarming with hummingbirds, and I got several nice images showing the buzz of activity. The middle of the day, which is the hottest, was spent moving from one location to another to get ready for the evening photo session. The evenings were spent setting up for nighttime photography of bats and other small mammals. On this trip, I tried to concentrate on photographing bats getting a drink of water from a small pond in the middle of the parched desert. It involved setting up many flash units (some installed just inches over the water's surface), all connected to some amazingly complicated electronics. The image I was after was bats taking a drink of water. After feeding on a huge variety of insects, bats need to wash it all down with a drink of water. The bats would fly down and skim the surface of a small pond and grab a quick drink. Using an infrared beam of light, the bats themselves would trigger the flash and camera, capturing the drinking action. I got several nice images of this behavior.

However, none of this compared with something that happened one evening. I was working on photographing a Southern Grasshopper Mouse (*Onychomys torridus*). These are small compact mice with short tails that make a living by eating, as you guessed, grasshoppers and other insects. They are the most carnivorous (insectivorous) of all the mice.

But this was not the cool part. Grasshopper mice are well known to stand on their hind legs, throw their heads back and howl like a wolf. Well, not exactly like a wolf. They sound more like a mouse, but I think you get the idea. Both the male and female do this behavior.

About two years ago, I was in the desert working on photographing grasshopper mice when I thought I saw one stand up, throw its head back and howl. What I heard was an extremely high-pitched, thin whistle, but I wasn't positive. On this trip while trying to photograph one, I had my back turned to the mouse. I suddenly heard a very high-pitched, thin whistle that almost hurt my ears. Immediately I remembered the sound from two years ago. I spun around and there was this grasshopper mouse. As I watched, he would scamper over to a small rock, climb on top, throw his head back and give his mouse-like wolf howl. I spent the next several hours photographing him/her howling. Head back and mouth open. You can't image how thrilled I was to finally see and photograph something that I had read about, but had never actually seen or even known anyone who had seen it.

(continued)

What role this howling accomplished, I don't know. But as a naturalist and wildlife photographer, every encounter that is documented in pictures and experiences adds to the overall body of scientific knowledge.

I wrapped up my adventure in the desert with many hours of hummingbird photography and headed for home completely exhausted from lack of sleep and way too much fun.

Turtle Season

It's turtle time of year! The time when turtles are seen crossing roads, traversing backyards—and are just about anywhere else you might look.

Once I was stopped at a traffic light, and I looked to my left. A large truck towing an even larger trailer was skidding to a stop in the turn lane. In front of the truck, a large snapping turtle was crossing the road. When the truck stopped, the passenger door flew open, a guy jumped out, trotted up to the snapper, grabbed it by the tail, walked to the roadside and released it into a small pond. I thought to myself, turtles could use more friends like these! I've actually done this very thing carefully hundreds of times over the years. Maybe you have, too.

So what are turtles doing when they're crossing roads and wandering in backyards? Well, most likely they are female turtles looking for a place to lay their eggs.

Turtles spend most of their life in water. During spring and early summer, male turtles seek out females for mating. In most species, the males tend to be slightly smaller and have extra long front claws, which help them hold on to the edges of the female's upper shell during mating. Males also have a concave area on their lower shell (plastron) that fits over the domed upper shell (carapace) of the female.

After the male mounts the female, a sperm packet is passed, which fertilizes the developing eggs. The female has a short window of time to find a suitable place to dig a nest and lay her eggs. Unlike birds, turtles don't incubate their eggs. Instead, they leave it to the sun-warmed earth to do the incubation.

A female turtle will leave her lake or pond and travel up to a half mile until she finds soil that is soft enough to dig an egg chamber. Sandy soil is often chosen since it's easy to excavate. Using only her back legs and feet, the female starts the digging process by wetting the soil with extra water she has stored in her bladder. She digs the nest chamber one scoop at a time with each of her hind feet—a slow process that she can't see because the work completed is behind her. If she is disturbed during this time, she will abandon the site and head back to the water.

In most species of turtles, the underground nest chamber temperature during incubation determines the sex of the offspring. Generally, warmer nests incubating at around 84–87 degrees produce mainly females. Cooler nests at 76–77 degrees produce mainly males. Nests incubating at 82–84 degrees produce a mix of females and males.

The nest chamber of a painted turtle is no deeper than 3–6 inches, or the depth at which the female can reach with her hind feet. Into the chamber she will deposit 5–20 pink-to-white leathery eggs. One time I watched a female painted turtle dig a chamber and lay six eggs in less than 30 minutes! Once a female starts laying eggs, she usually won't be scared off and is completely vulnerable to predators.

When the eggs are deposited, the female takes great care to backfill the chamber with dirt and tamp it down. She will even move debris over the site to camouflage the location. Afterward, the female typically makes a beeline back to the safety of the water. Females may have several nests in one season, but usually several days or weeks pass between each nesting.

Now it's up to the sun to warm the earth and incubate the eggs. This is the dangerous time. Most studies show that 70–90 percent of all turtle nests are predated by raccoons, skunks, domestic cats and dogs, opossums, foxes, coyotes and nearly any other animal that has a nose good enough to smell buried eggs.

The length of incubation for painted turtles is 70–80 days, so eggs laid now won't hatch until September or October. If the weather is good when the young hatch, they will emerge from the chamber in autumn and head directly to the lake. Young turtles hatching later, however, will remain in their underground nest until the following spring before heading to the lake, where the entire process starts all over again.

Skinks

Every time I mention to people that we have lizards living in Minnesota, I get the same crazy looks as when I tell them we have cacti growing here also. Both seem extremely unlikely in a place where winter often lasts longer than the summer.

Skinks are reptiles, closely related to snakes. The first reptiles evolved about 330 million years ago, shortly after the amphibians (frogs and salamanders), which were some of the earliest vertebrates to inhabit the land. The earliest reptiles were small lizards, which later became the well-known dinosaurs. Current-day lizards evolved about 2 million years ago.

Skinks are small lizards in the Scincidae family. It is the third-largest lizard family, with nearly 1,200 species worldwide. There are 14 skink species in North America. They all have smooth, scaled-covered bodies with short legs and long tails.

The Prairie Skink (*Eumeces septentrionalis*) is about 5–7 inches long, including the tail—approximately half of the total length consists of the tail. It's brown to black with several light tan stripes running down the back. It has short powerful legs and a pointed snout that enable it to burrow quickly into the soil headfirst. It is also a very fast runner on the surface.

Young hatchlings are around half the size of adults. They are also brown with light stripes running down their backs, but they have very unique bright blue tails. The blue color is not the only unique aspect of a skink's tail. The Prairie Skink has the ability to detach or disjoint its tail when grasped by a predator, leaving behind a wiggling tail segment that acts as a decoy while the skink scurries under a rock or burrows into the soil. The loss of the tail is only a minor inconvenience because it grows back in just 4–10 weeks. However, the new tail will never reach the length of the original tail.

As the name implies, Prairie Skinks live in prairies, preferring sunny locations with plenty of grass and other vegetation for cover. They like loose sandy soils in which to burrow. They also like rocks and logs to hide beneath.

In regions that get snow, skinks overwinter below the frost line in burrows that they dig for themselves. Early each spring, the skinks become active, sunning themselves in the warm sunshine. Although they are active throughout summer and into early fall, they are one of the most secretive animals. Rarely will you see them unless you are searching.

Breeding males often have a bright red-to-orange chin and throat. Mating takes place in early spring. After breeding, the females will dig a nest under a rock or log and lay up to 10 white, leathery eggs that measure only ½ inch in diameter. The eggs will expand slightly to be around ¾ inch near hatching time.

Incubation takes about 40–50 days, depending on the soil tempera-ture. The sun warms the soil, which in turn incubates the eggs. The female skink will guard the eggs until the young hatch. She will stay with the young for several days after hatching to help protect them. Now that is a good lizard mother!

Condors at the Canyon

This column comes from the South Rim of the Grand Canyon, where I am fortunate enough to have an opportunity to see and photograph the largest flying bird in the United States—the incredible California Condor.

I was here shortly after the initial reintroduction of the condor to northern Arizona, so I was interested in seeing how the largest bird in North America was doing. The condor reintroduction goal was to release enough of these prehistoric birds in northern Arizona and southern Utah to establish a breeding population. This way if a disease or natural disaster occurred within the main population of condors in California, there would be a healthy gene pool to draw from to repopulate.

But first, a little history about the condor. During the height of the last ice age, around 10,000–50,000 years ago, condors flew over the land in search of carcasses of huge animals such as the Ground Sloth and Woolly Mammoth. Condor bones dating back to the ice age have been recovered in several Grand Canyon caves. For unknown reasons, sometime after the ice age the condors disappeared from the Grand Canyon. By the time the European settlement occurred, condors were found only along the Pacific Coast from Canada to Baja California.

By the 1800s, the remaining condor population began to drop due to a variety of reasons. Not surprisingly, most were human related. By the early 1920s, it was estimated that fewer than 100 condors were in existence. By the 1980s, there were only 22 California Condors left in the world. Something needed to be done or the extinction of the largest bird species in North America was at hand. The decision was made to capture the remaining wild birds and bring them into captivity.

A very successful captive breeding program was launched and soon there were enough condors to start to release back into the wild. The first releases of the condor occurred in central California, where the original birds were captured. The second population was started in late 1996, when six condors were released in Arizona. Since then, several captive-bred birds have been released each year. Since all of the released birds were youngsters and condors don't start to breed until they are 5–6 years of age, the first wild breeding attempt didn't occur until the early 2000s. Predictably, the first wild breeding attempts were not successful, but in 2003 the first wild condor chick hatched. This was a huge milestone in the recovery of this most amazing bird.

Although all nesting attempts in 2006 were not successful, the breeding season for 2007 looked bright. Since these birds nest deep within caves located high up in canyon walls, it was difficult to monitor exactly what was going on. Researchers suspected successful hatching in two nests. They based their assumption of the successful hatching of chicks by the number of adults in the nest site cave.

Today there are a total of 59 condors in northern Arizona and a grand total of 290 California Condors in existence. This makes the condor the most endangered bird species in North America. Presently all living condors are tagged and have radio transmitters affixed to their wings.

Enough history—let's turn back to the South Rim. The sun is shining and temperatures are in the mid 80s with a slight wind out of the north. I am standing just a couple feet from the edge of a cliff that drops nearly 1,000 feet to the bottom of the Grand Canyon. I have been standing here since 8 a.m. It was now nearly noon and my stomach was rumbling in anticipation of lunch. Out over the pine forest I spot an adult condor heading my way. Using the updrafts, the condor soars effortlessly and silently on its massive 9-foot wingspan. It's an adult bird and it starts to turn and bank, sending him on a course directly toward me. I focus my camera and begin capturing some amazing images.

A family on vacation with several small children suddenly step up to ask me what I am photographing at the exact time this huge adult condor swings by us at eye level no less than 30 feet away. I am firing away with my camera as the family suddenly sees what I am photographing. All together the family gives a chorus of, "WHOA— LOOK AT THAT BIRD!" They ask me what that huge bird was. I tell them they just got an up-close and personal look at the largest and most endangered bird in North America—the California Condor. What a great experience for me, and especially for that family.

Rainbows

One day a fast-moving and strong late afternoon thunderstorm interrupted my tinkering in our perennial flower gardens. The storm quickly passed and the sun came out again. I mentioned to my wife that these conditions were perfect for one of nature's more impressive visual displays, an atmospheric spectral light display otherwise known as a rainbow.

We headed out past the gardens to an open place between the trees. We stood with the sun at our backs and scanned the distant sky that was still pouring some rain. Sure enough, there it was—a rainbow, as big and bright as can be.

Rainbows are very special. They are one of those natural events that should be celebrated and shared with friends and family. They are truly one of nature's most magnificent shows. They rate right up there with blazing orange and red sunsets.

For all their grandness, rainbows are actually very simple. You can recreate one with just the spray from your garden hose and a little afternoon sunshine. But what makes all those colors?

When you see a rainbow you are actually seeing bent sunlight. The sunlight enters a falling raindrop and is reflected to come out the same side of the raindrop, except it's now broken into the full light spectrum, kind of like a prism. It's all a matter of bending sunlight.

Rainbows occur only when sunlight shines in one part of the sky and rain falls in the opposite part of the sky. The only way you can see a rainbow is to face the rainy part of the sky and have the sun at your back. Storms (rain) tend to travel from west to east in our area. Because of this, a rainbow in the evening indicates the storm has passed and clear weather is forecasted, and a rainbow in the morning suggests a storm is coming. The old saying "Red sky at night, sailor's delight; red sky in morning, sailor take warning" holds true for the very same reasons.

Bending light is called refracting. In the case of rainbows, not all sunlight is refracted. Most

Every aspect of each rainbow, such as shape, intensity and duration, is unique—so enjoy all the rainbows that you are fortunate enough to see!

of the sunlight passes right through the raindrop and is seen as regular sunlight. Only a small portion of light is reflected when it strikes the backside of the droplet. This light is refracted (bent) as it passes both into and out of the raindrop, and is returned to our eyes as the colors of a rainbow.

Because each light ray bends differently from the rest, each ray of light emerges from the drop at a slightly different angle. When the light exits the raindrop, it is dispersed into the spectrum of visible light or colors from red to violet. An easy way to remember the full spectrum of visible light is by the acronym ROY-G-BIV. Each letter stands for one color in the full spectrum of visible light—red, orange, yellow, green, blue, indigo and violet.

Furthermore, we see only a single light color from each raindrop. Because of this, it takes millions of raindrops to create a single rainbow. If you move, you will see a completely different ray of light from each drop, thus a completely different rainbow. The rainbow you see is not the same as the one the person standing next to you is seeing. In effect, the rainbow you see is your own personal light bow.

Northern Lights

It was sometime past midnight. I was on a lakeshore in northern Minnesota with my digital audio recorder and parabolic microphone in hand, waiting to record the nightly serenade of resident loons. I wanted to record the four distinct vocalizations of the Common Loon, but what I got instead was a streaming curtain of light across the northern sky—the shimmering aurora!

The word "aurora" comes from the Roman goddess of the dawn, Aurora. The name was given to the spectacle of light that appears in the skies near our polar regions. In the Northern Hemisphere, the lights are called aurora borealis, or northern lights. In the Southern Hemisphere, they are called aurora australis, or southern lights.

Auroras are caused by the sun. Sometimes the sun has violent storms, during which a stream of charged particles (plasma) is spewed out in an event called a coronal mass ejection. The result of the storms are solar winds filled with highly charged, tiny particles traveling at speeds of 1–2 million miles per hour.

It takes 2–3 days for the solar winds to reach our planet. When the particles arrive, they are drawn toward the North and South Poles by Earth's magnetic field. The particles hit and interact with our atmosphere, and the sky begins to glow.

The delicate colors of the auroras depend on the height at which the energy particles collide with our atmosphere. Street lamps and neon signs emit different colors of light, depending on the gas types trapped in the fixtures. The same applies to the auroras. If the predominant gases are oxygen and nitrogen, the auroras will be red. This event is rare and happens only at times of maximum solar activity. The most common color is green, and then yellow—again, caused by oxygen, but at lower levels.

Auroras happen at any time, but the peak occurs at 27-day intervals (auroral activity is based on our sun's rotation and solar activity) and usually lasts for several nights in a row. Northern lights glowing just after dark are not very showy. The best displays are around midnight or shortly after.

Auroras are never absent from the earth. Every hour of the day, every day of the year, they are blazing somewhere on the planet. However, most people can go for years without seeing the display, because the aurora spends most of its time around the far ends of the earth—where there are lots of penguins and polar bears, but few humans.

The best place to view auroras is within an auroral zone. The auroral zone in the north includes the polar regions from Alaska through the Canadian Northwest Territories, around to Norway, through Russia and back to Alaska. Along this band, the lights can be seen on virtually every cloudless night from fall to spring. Small expansions of the auroral zone are common and the aurora will often spill out into neighboring areas.

Oh, and by the way—the loons never called that night. I think they were speechless, as was I, just watching the light show unfold above.

Meteor Showers

Go ahead and pay seven or eight dollars for a movie. For my money, the summer's blockbuster is the Perseid meteor shower—and it's free. The Perseid meteor shower is one of eight major meteor showers that light up the night sky each year.

Starting in January, the Quadrantid meteor shower gives us a brief, but intense, shower. April brings the Lyrid meteor shower and May is the time for Eta Aquarid. Delta Aquarid can be seen in July or August. October, November and December each have a shower visible to the night sky watcher.

The Perseid meteor shower is an annual event that lasts several days in August. It has been better than usual over the last few years because the comet responsible for the cosmic dust and debris that produces meteors recently swept through our region of the solar system. When the Perseid occurs in a new moon phase (when there's no moonlight to interfere with the view), it promises to be one of the best meteor shows of the year.

What most people call shooting or falling stars are really meteors. Meteors aren't falling stars in the sense of stars actually falling from the sky to Earth. Our closest star is the sun. Now imagine the sun falling to Earth and you can see the absurdity of the phrase.

All meteor showers are named after the constellation in which they appear to originate in the night sky. The Perseid shower is so obvious that all you have to do is look up to see the show. You can expect to see several shooting stars approximately every five minutes.

Meteor showers are the result of comets. Comets are very large, dirty snowballs orbiting the sun like the rest of the planets. As comets travel though space, they leave behind a trail of cosmic dust and debris. When comets are observed from Earth, they appear like a glowing ball with a long tail, much like a kite with a long tail stretched out behind.

Whizzing though space, following its normal path around the sun, Earth passes though the cosmic litter left behind by the comet each August. Most cosmic particles are only about the size of a grain of sand, but each has an enormous impact on our atmosphere.

There are many comets in our solar system, each leaving behind remnants. Whenever Earth passes through one of these bands of debris, they interact with Earth's atmosphere. The friction of the debris with the atmosphere produces heat of such intense temperature that the bits of debris begin to glow. What we see are bright flashes of light racing across the sky as the debris burns up.

The speed at which meteors fall varies. A casual observer will be able to see the difference between fast and slow meteors. The difference is all in the direction in which the meteors impact our atmosphere. Earth revolves in a counterclockwise direction around the sun at 18½ miles per second. Meteor particles travel at a faster rate of 25 miles per second.

Slow meteors are those that impact Earth's atmosphere while traveling in the same direction as the revolving Earth. Thus, they impact our atmosphere at a reduced speed of 6½ miles per second (25-18½=6½). They have faint, luminous tails. Fast meteors appear as quick streaks and impact our atmosphere in the opposite direction that Earth is revolving. Their speed plus the speed at which Earth is moving into them equals 43½ miles per second (25+18½=43½).

On clear nights, the Perseid meteor show is worth staying up to see. Grab your favorite lawn chair and bug spray and head out after dark to see the summer's best natural show.

Summer Feeding Frenzy

On a trip to the far reaches of northern Minnesota for Black Bears, I had a chance to photograph bears in their end-of-summer feeding frenzy. They were so intent on feeding, the challenge was not finding them—it was getting them to lift up their heads long enough for a good picture.

There are three species of bears in North America. The Polar Bear, Grizzly Bear and Black Bear. The Black Bear (*Ursus americanus*) is the most common and widespread bear in North America. It ranges across the northern states and Canada from coast to coast, with the range reaching like fingers down the Appalachian Mountains as far south as Florida and down the Rocky Mountains to Mexico. In addition, there are pockets of bears found in many southern states. Overall, the population of Black Bears is growing all across the nation.

Each spring Black Bears emerge from their winter dens and begin to feed. They have lost so much weight over winter that it is very important to find enough food to regain their strength and energy in preparation for mating. Mating season starts in late May and extends into early July.

Summer is a good time of year for bears. Mating is over and living is good. Foraging for food and milling around their home range take up much of their time. Insects are plentiful and their favorite food, green grasses and sedges, are everywhere. Plants make up 80 percent of the diet.

Beginning in late August, a Black Bear's hormones kick into high gear, which in turn starts the bears on a feeding frenzy. In order for a bear to survive 5–6 months of winter dormancy, it needs to have a sufficient layer of fat from which the body draws its energy. Without enough fat stored, the bear may not make it to the following spring. In addition, the amount and quality of the fat will determine if and how many cubs a mother bear will have during the coming winter.

Black Bears occur only in North America. They inhabit forested regions, but can also be found in mountainous places, open tundra and more and more in suburban areas. There are an estimated 750,000 Black Bears in the United States.

Although bears mate in June, the prospective mother will not actually become pregnant until November. This is called delayed implantation and is fairly common in large mammals such as bears. So if a mother bear is healthy and has an adequate fat layer going into winter dormancy, she will give birth to several (usually 2) cubs in January or early February. If she is not carrying enough fat she will not have any cubs.

So in preparation for the coming winter, all bears at this time of year are in a hyperactive eating mode called hyperphagia. This leads to bears feeding for up to 20 hours a day, taking in huge amounts of calories. Most of the foodstuff is in the form of plants, but they also eat as many insects, berries and nuts as they can find. Years with droughts, which result in few berries and nuts and are tough on bears, force them to find alternative food sources. This causes them to break into cabins, tear down bird feeders and raid garbage cans. The bears are so single-minded on eating at this time of year that they sleep only a couple hours each day. The rest of the time is devoted to foraging for food. Some bears may travel hundreds of miles in search of a rich food supply.

Nectar-feeding Marathon

Glancing at the old, rusted mercury-filled thermometer tacked to the wooden post, I could see that it was 101 degrees. And the worst part is, I am standing in the shade. A temperature above 100 is fairly normal for southeastern Arizona in August, which is where I am now. I'm here at the hottest time of year to photograph some special critters—hummingbirds and nectar-feeding bats. In August, both hummers and bats are at their highest numbers because they migrate through this part of Arizona on their way south into Mexico.

During this blazing hot afternoon I am photographing humming-birds, but after sundown I'll be photographing bats. This is how it goes, day after day for the past five days. Up until 1–2 a.m. with the bats at night, then get a few hours of sleep before waking at 5 a.m. to photograph hummers.

In the eastern half of the country there is only one hummingbird species—the Ruby-throated Hummingbird. It is a hardy species that has managed to colonize the entire half of the country, and well up into Canada. Here in Arizona there are 18 species of hummingbirds. About eight of these are fairly widespread and occur throughout the western half of the country. The rest are highly specialized and occur only in the southeastern corner of Arizona. These specialized species occur mainly in the tropics of Mexico and extend northward, just barely reaching into the United States in Arizona. This great diversity of hummingbirds is the reason I am here.

I am set up in the shade of a structure that has a large corrugated metal roof and no walls. Just six tall wooden poles hold up the roof. It took nearly a day to set up all four flashes and work out the details of the camera and flash settings to take pictures of hummingbirds. The object is to take hummingbird pictures and "freeze" their wings to look perfectly still while the bird is in flight. You see, if you take a regular picture of a hummingbird while in flight, its wings flap so fast that not even my camera's fast shutter speed is quick enough to stop the rapid motion of the wings. In the amount of time that my camera's shutter opens, allows enough light in to expose the image and then closes, the hummer's wings have flapped about a dozen times, creating an image of blurred wings.

So what I am doing is fooling the camera by photographing in the shade. I have set up the four high-speed flashes to use as my primary light source. And now for the tricky part. I have set the flashes to give off a lot of light, but only for a very short duration of time—about $\frac{1}{3200}$ of a second. So when a hummingbird comes in and feeds at some flowers and I push the shutter release in the relative darkness of the shade, the camera's shutter opens and the high-speed flashes go off. Only the short blast of light exposes the image, not the daylight. In other words, the camera sees only what the flashes light up for that incredibly short moment of time, and voilà—an image of a hummingbird with frozen wings.

I love photographing hummingbirds partly because hummingbirds are one of my favorite birds and also for the challenge they bring to making beautiful pictures. Hummingbirds are so very different from other birds, and I love their quickness and agility. I also enjoy how they buzz from one flower to the next, sipping the tiniest drop of nectar. What's not to admire about this tiny bird?

Bats are another great story. In the United States we have about 45 different species of bats, but here in southeastern Arizona I'm interested in just two of these bats—nectar-feeding bats known as the Mexican Long-tongued Bat and the Lesser Long-nosed Bat. These are some of the smallest of all living mammals and weigh under 10 grams. They are highly specialized bats, feeding mainly on the nectar of desert-blooming plants.

Most bats feed mainly on insects and small reptiles and amphibians. In fact, bats eat so many insects that a world without bats would be overrun by flying bugs. Nectar-feeding bats also eat insects, but they feed heavily on the high-energy nectar and pollen of night-blooming plants. They can ingest up to 150 percent of their body weight in nectar each night.

Nectar-feeding bats live in Mexico and Central America and migrate thousands of miles to follow the blooming flowers of specific plants such as the saguaro cactus and agave. In spring the bats migrate north out of Mexico, following the bloom of saguaro cacti. The saguaro is a very large cactus that stands up to 30 feet tall with upward bent arms. It's the signature plant of the southwestern desert. Each spring, saguaros produce

Bats have been migrating for hundreds of thousands of years. They feed primarily on flower nectar, but they'll also stop at hummingbird feeders along the way.

clusters of large white flowers that bloom at night and attract the bats. This cactus depends on the bats for pollination. In fact, more than 300 plants, such as mangoes, bananas and agave, are pollinated only by bats.

By the end of summer, the bats have reached the southern quarter of Arizona, where the saguaro's range stops and its flowers have stopped blooming. Now the bats turn and head south, returning to Mexico. This time they follow the blooming of agave plants, which flower from the end of August through September. Again, the agave plants depend on these bats for pollination just as the bats depend on the agaves for food.

My timing is perfect, because the bats showed up on their southward migration just three days before I arrived. An hour past sunset, when the evening fades into complete darkness, the bats start flying in search of blooming agave flowers. I have set up my camera and three flashes on a large agave flower. I am using a wonderful device called the Phototrap, which uses an infrared beam of light to trigger my camera. Since it's dark and I can't see the bats, I am relying on my Phototrap to "see" the bats and trigger my camera and flashes. About an hour passes before my camera suddenly goes off and the flashes light up the night sky. For a split second I can see the bat visiting my flower in the glare of the flashes.

Even though it's dark, it is still very warm and the insects are a bit annoying. It is still so warm that the sweat of the day hasn't dried on my brow. I sit and wait in the darkness until 2 a.m. before giving up for the night and heading to bed. I'm so darn tired that I will have to wait until morning to look at my images. But it was well worth the time and effort.

Autumn

Sphinx Moths

I have many favorite visitors to my naturalist garden. First and fore-most are the Ruby-throated Hummingbirds. These flying jewels thrill me to no end. Next are all the different kinds of butterflies—Red Admirals, Tiger Swallowtails, Mourning Cloaks, Monarchs and Viceroys. They flitter into my garden and my heart. But the for-sure "wow" power—the sphinx moth—is the real garden show-stopper!

Sphinx moths, also called hawk moths or hummingbird moths, are large moths that many gardeners confuse with hummingbirds. These daytime and evening moths have a 3½-inch wingspan, making them nearly as large as Ruby-throats.

There are about 100 species of sphinx moths in North America. One of the more common is the White-lined Sphinx Moth (*Hyles lineata*). This whirling moth has a buff-brown body (thorax and abdomen) with large pointed brown forewings outlined with white lines or stripes, and mostly pink hind wings. It also has six white lines on its thorax, which is where the wings attach. The abdomen looks like the tail and has black and white spots separated by three pale pink lines.

The White-lined flaps its wings so fast, it's hard to see the white stripes. Some sphinx moth species can flap their wings up to 85 beats per second and fly up to 10 miles per hour. That might be slow for a hum-mingbird, but it's very fast for a moth.

Another common sphinx moth is the smaller Green-banded Sphinx Moth. It's about twice the size of a bumblebee, with three bright green bands on its abdomen. Some mistake these moths for baby hummingbirds.

A sphinx moth will hover at flowers for nectar just like a humming-bird. It has a long straw-like mouth, called a proboscis, which is usually coiled under its head like a spring. The proboscis is very long—usually about the length of the moth's entire body. When the moth approaches a flower, it uncoils the proboscis and inserts it into the flower, like a straw into a milkshake. It quickly sips the nectar and moves to another flower.

Sphinx moths have large eyes to see flowers, but lack ears and can't hear. One way to tell the difference between a sphinx moth and a hummingbird is to use your ears. Hummingbirds make a loud humming noise when flying—that's how they got their name. Sphinx moths are silent.

Before any moth can fly, it first has to go through a caterpillar stage. The caterpillar of the sphinx moth is very large, about 3 inches long and about as thick as your little finger. It's usually bright green with a large horn on its tail, which gives a threatening appearance, but is harmless. At this stage the caterpillar is often called a hornworm. When disturbed, it typically rears up to an imposing posture with its head cocked, reminding some people of the great Egyptian Sphinx—and hence the common name.

Unlike other moths, the sphinx moth caterpillar doesn't spin a silken cocoon to metamorphose, but burrows underground, creating a protective earthen chamber. The buried chamber is also how it survives winter.

Molting Time

It's molting time again. No, this isn't a sad country music song—it's what is happening with our backyard birds right now. At the end of summer and early fall most birds are molting. It's not a bad thing. It is when the birds replace their old worn-out feathers with new ones.

Molting can be described as an orderly replacement of a bird's feathers. There are a couple different kinds of molts. Complete molts are when all feathers on a bird's body, wings and tail are replaced. This is a slow, orderly process of replacing just a few feathers at a time. It doesn't hinder the bird from flying or change its appearance and it usually takes place symmetrically. For example, when the third primary flight feather is replaced on one wing, it's replaced at the same time on the opposite wing.

Partial molts involve only the large contour feathers on a bird's body, and not the wings and tail. Birds that partially molt have two molts per year: one molt for the body alone and one for the body, wings and tail. Molts are usually spaced out about halfway through each year.

All birds molt, but molts vary greatly from species to species. Some birds, such as the American Crow, molt only one complete molt per year. At this time of year, adult crows replace all of their feathers one by one and grow new replacement feathers. It is a slow process and since it's only a couple feathers at a time, most people don't notice it. Sometimes you can see old worn-out feathers next to shiny new feathers, but that's about the extent of it.

American Goldfinches undergo a complete molt in late September. The males lose their bright yellow and black feathers and replace them with dull green feathers. They will undergo a partial molt in spring and return to their bright canary yellow and black colors. This usually starts in later winter.

Only a handful of birds have two complete molts per year. These birds live in challenging habitats and wear out their feathers very quickly. These include Marsh Wrens and Bobolinks. They live in environments with rough vegetation, which wears out feathers faster than open habitats.

Some species of birds have just one complete molt each year. However, like the American Goldfinch, they will change colors over the year, which seems a little contradictory. The European Starling is one of these birds. In early autumn they appear to be covered with white and brown spots. Gone is the dark, sleek coat of black feathers that shines purple and green in summer sunlight. During fall and winter the starlings look completely different—so much so that I've had people contact me and ask if they have some new bird in their yard because they hadn't seen this spotted bird before.

The brown and white spots of the starling are only on the tips of the feathers and appear right after their one complete molt in late summer. During fall and winter the tips of the feathers wear off, and by spring all spots are gone, leaving the bird in its sleek coat of black feathers. It's a complete transformation from worn-away feather tips, but no molting.

The Northern Cardinal is the same way. In fall and early winter the male cardinals undergo a complete molt and replace all of their worn red feathers. However, if you look closely in the winter, they have a tinge of gray, especially on the back. That is because all of their new feathers have gray edges. The gray edge wears off during the rigors of winter, and by springtime the male cardinal will again look bright red and be ready to impress the girls without having to go through another complete molt.

Another molt cardinals are doing at this time is replacing their head feathers, which produces a lot of "bald" cardinals. Both the males and females drop all of their head fathers at the same time, exposing their dark skin beneath. This is another phenomenon that I am contacted about on a regular basis. One time I had three cardinals coming to my feeders and all were missing their head feathers. It takes just a couple weeks to grow the feathers back and return the cardinals to their former beauty.

Whooping Delight

I step out of my truck into the cold predawn darkness. I see nothing, but I can hear a great diversity of birds. Immediately I hear a pair of Great Horned Owls hooting back and forth no more than a hundred yards away. In the distance is the honking of a flock of Canada Geese. I can also hear dozens of Sandhill Cranes sounding off with their ancient bone-rattling call. But it is none of these birds that I am in Wisconsin to see and photograph. No, I'm here for a very special and rare bird, the Whooping Crane.

I am writing from the Necedah National Wildlife Refuge. It is Wisconsin's largest federally owned refuge consisting of over 44,000 acres, but when you count the adjacent federally managed land it totals a whopping 114,000 acres. Needless to say, it's a wildlife haven.

Refuge manager Larry Wargowsky tells me "this place is really an endangered species refuge" because it is home to three high-profile endangered species—the Karner Blue Butterfly, the Eastern Gray Wolf and the Whooping Crane. Larry tells me that this large continuous block of habitat allows uncommon species, such as the Fisher and North American Porcupine, along with wolves and bears, to live farther south in Wisconsin than they would normally occur. I can bear witness to that because I saw and photographed one of the wolves early this morning.

With over 5,000 acres of wetlands and impoundments (large shallow lakes), this refuge was selected to be the place where an experimental free-flying flock of endangered Whooping Cranes would be established. After years of planning, the project released its first cranes in 2001. Young cranes were raised by Operation Migration (OM) staff members, who dressed in costumes and mimicked adult cranes. Each year about 8–21 young cranes are trained at this facility and are taught to fly behind an ultralight aircraft to learn how to migrate. I am sure this is not the first time you've heard about this amazing story. By all means of measurement, this project to establish a migrating flock of Whooping Cranes has been a success. But one spring, disaster struck when nearly all of the young cranes raised and flown to Florida were killed in a freak accident—a tornado.

Setbacks are part of any success story, but they are usually never the end of the story. And the Whooping Crane project is no exception. Staff from OM told me that 35 Whooping Crane eggs were hatched during spring in preparation for the upcoming class. Seventeen of those crane chicks were learning how to eat and drink at the facility—and most importantly, fly and migrate by following the ultralight.

I had a chance to spend a couple days with the staff of OM to see firsthand how this process was working. Weeks before my arrival, the staff of OM had spent hundreds of hours feeding and training the young cranes. This involved dressing in an all-white costume and handholding a lifelike head of an adult Whooping Crane to feed the young birds. Now standing almost as tall as their parents, the young cranes are learning to fly and follow the ultralight aircraft.

Each morning just as the sun is peeking over the horizon, pilots from OM take off from their hanger and land at the holding pens of the young cranes. The young birds are released from their protective enclosure and immediately start to stretch their wings and dance about. It doesn't take too much encouragement to get the young birds to follow the aircraft. Within a minute they are off and flying. They make several circles and land again. All total, they are airborne for about 25 minutes. The young birds are returned to the holding area—another successful flight.

This goes on day after day (weather providing) until October, when it's time to migrate south. All the months of preparation pay off when the pilots and support staff take off and head south with the ultimate destination being Florida, where they will spend the winter.

Interestingly, the Whooping Cranes need only to be shown the way down to Florida once. After that the birds will return to central Wisconsin on their own, where they will spend the summer and hopefully repro-duce, thus establishing a free-flying, migratory flock of the endangered Whooping Crane.

Coons

I have known many raccoons over the years and each one was a delight. I find their inquisitive nature much like my own and their intelligence nearly unmatched among other wild animals. Raccoons are also one of our most unmistakable critters. Their black mask and bushy, ringed tail makes identification quick and easy. Their coat is often grizzled gray, but it can be brown to nearly black or, in rare cases, pure white. They have short ears, a long white snout and they waddle when they walk.

Raccoons are in the Procyonidae family. Interestingly, this family is found only in North and South America—the New World. Their only close relative outside the New World is the panda of Southeast Asia. However, the classification of the Giant Panda is in dispute.

Raccoons are found in every part of North America except for the higher elevations of the Rocky Mountains and parts of the desert Southwest. They are usually associated with forests where they use trees for dens, but now they occur in just about any habitat, even in the treeless prairie where they will den underground. Raccoons are one of the few animals that have benefited from urban sprawl. In most places they are much more common now than they were 40–50 years ago.

Adult raccoons are solitary critters, except when the mother has young. Mating occurs in early spring and gestation lasts 54–63 days. Females give birth to 3–6 young near the end of May. The mother leads the young away from the den by the middle of July. This is when some raccoons end up flattened on the road. The babies stay with their mother for nearly a year.

They spend the rest of the summer sleeping during the day and moving around at night in search of food. They find a new place to sleep each night. The goal is to build layers of fat that will allow them to enter a winter sleep—not a true hibernation. In northern states with cold winters, at about the end of October most raccoons enter a deep sleep, called torpor, and awaken in mid-February. Males usually overwinter on their own, while the females den with their young. However, there are reports of several males overwintering together.

Raccoons are true omnivores, which means they will eat both plant and animal material. It's not uncommon for a coon to eat bird eggs, baby birds, crayfish, fish, acorns, berries and green leaves. They also love birdseed. While they prefer black-oil sunflower seeds, they don't hesitate to eat thistle, safflower, millet and suet. Raccoons often outwit homeowners and rob them of the seeds they've put out for the birds. My feeling is if you put out free food for birds, you shouldn't be surprised when a masked bandit shows up in the middle of the night and helps itself to dinner.

Porcupines

There are many unusual animals in nature. There's a squirrel that can nearly fly (glide) with just a little extra skin stretched between its legs. Snakes can quickly scoot along the ground and even climb trees without legs. And then there is the porcupine. It is certainly one of the most unusual critters in the woods.

The North American Porcupine (*Erethizon dorsatum*) is a large, stout, grizzled-looking rodent. It is most famous for its sharp spines and quills, but beyond that, most people don't know much about these unusual critters.

Porcupines, like all animals, are covered with a dense short underfur (hair) that gives them their dark color. They also have long guard hairs that are tipped with white, which accounts for the grizzled appearance. Their famous quills or spines are located only on the rump or tail, not all over their bodies as most people think.

Each spine is simply a modified (stiff) guard hair. It is covered with microscopic scales near the tip, which act like barbs. When a quill penetrates into flesh, the tiny scales make it extremely difficult to remove.

Porcupines also have long, sharp claws that allow them to climb trees. Like other rodents, they have sharp incisor teeth (two front teeth on the top and bottom) that continuously grow. Gnawing on wood helps to keep the teeth from growing too large. Porcupines are also known for gnawing on other wooden objects such as ax handles and outbuilding plywood.

Porcupines range from Mexico up through most of the western United States, into Alaska and east to New England. They are usually found in coniferous forests (pine), but they also live in scrubby areas with only deciduous trees.

Unlike other rodents, which reproduce quickly and live only a short time, porcupines reproduce very slowly and live a long time. It just goes to show that there is always an exception to the rules in nature. Gestation lasts over 200 days (approximately 6½ months), and each mother has only one baby per year. Not all mothers produce a baby every year. Most young are born in March or April and are fully furred with eyes open and can follow their mothers. They are born with a full complement of quills that harden shortly after birth.

Baby porcupines nurse for up to three months after birth, but can eat tree bark at two weeks of age. Adults eat the inner bark of tree branches. It appears that they are eating only the hard, dry outer bark, but they need to remove the outer bark to reach the soft, juicy inner bark. They prefer white pines over just about any other tree. You might think of porcupines as beavers that can climb trees. Both eat the soft bark of the upper branches, but only one climbs the tree. The other cuts it down.

Porcupines have lived more than 10 years in captivity. In the wild they usually live only about half as long. Even though they have sharp quills, many animals prey on porcupines. Lynx, bobcats, coyotes, martens, wolves and other predators will take a porcupine by knocking it off its feet and biting its soft belly. The predator only needs to stay away from the porcupine's tail. Porcupines are not good at defending themselves. They move very slowly, and it's not true that they can throw their quills.

You will see porcupines together only during mating season or when the young are with their mothers. They are usually nocturnal, sleeping in treetops during the day. They don't hibernate, but will sleep for a week at a time during winter. In winter they eat only the inner bark of trees. During spring and summer they often eat green plants and garden crops.

Nature is full of what I like to call "gee-whiz" stuff. The porcupine is one of those gee-whiz animals.

Acorn Nuttiness

Have you ever noticed that some years are better than others for acorns? Sometimes it seems like millions can be dropping from every oak tree.

Acorns are, of course, the seeds of oak trees. From the tiny acorn springs forth the mighty oak. They are produced by the tree's tiny flowers, which are wind-pollinated in spring. All oak trees produce separate male and female flowers on the same tree—a reproductive condition called monoecious. It is the female flower that will result in an acorn after it has been pollinated.

The caps of the acorn are a collection of overlapping modified leaves that protected the female flower before it blossomed. The acorn itself is the female flower's ovary that has grown and hardened with a protective shell around a single seed within.

The meat within the acorn is what nourishes the germinating seed until it can produce its first leaves. The acorn meat is kind of like the yolk in a bird's egg, which nourishes the developing chick within.

As you might imagine, acorns, just like eggs, are a very desirable food source for a lot of wildlife. Many birds, such as Wild Turkeys, Ruffed Grouse and Wood Ducks, feed heavily on acorns at this time of year. Each of these birds has a strong "upper stomach," called a gizzard, that enables them to swallow an acorn whole and grind it into digestible food.

Other birds, such as Blue Jays and some woodpeckers, will hammer an acorn shell open with their bills before eating the meat inside. Animals, such as Eastern Chipmunks and Red Squirrels, gather hundreds of acorns for winter storage. They simply and easily peel the shell open with their sharp incisor teeth to eat the seed within. Black Bears, Northern Raccoons and White-tailed Deer also eat acorns each fall. They use their strong molar teeth to grind the acorns before swallowing.

While many animals eat acorns, it's the Eastern Gray Squirrel that actually helps the oak tree. If you have ever watched a gray squirrel, you will notice how they find a single acorn and carry it off to bury it in a shallow hole, presumably for later consumption. Since it's impossible for the squirrels to remember all of their hidden treasures, the forgotten acorns (which have been "planted" at the ideal depth for germination) foster the next generation of oak trees.

All of our oak trees can be broken into two categories or groups. The first is the white oak group (or sometimes called black oak). These trees have flowers that produce acorns every year. Most years they produce a small to moderate amount of acorns per tree. However, once every 3–5 years and sometimes every other year, these trees produce huge crops of acorns. This is called a mass crop of acorns.

The second category is the red oak group. This group of trees produces acorns every other year. Red oak flowers are pollinated in the spring, but the acorns are not ripe until a year from the following autumn.

So how do you tell if your oak tree is in the white or red oak group? It's simple. Oaks that have leaves with rounded lobes are in the white oak group. Oaks with leaves that have sharp points are in the red oak group.

Autumn Colors

Who doesn't love it when the trees turn from their uniform green to the many shades of autumn? I know I do. The only thing that bothers me is how short the autumn colors can be. One good windy day or a heavy rainstorm and all the blaze and glory are gone—and we have to wait another year before it's back again.

Leaves are green because of a pigment known as chlorophyll. When chlorophyll is healthy and happy, it dominates any other pigment in the leaf. But chlorophyll doesn't just give leaves their color—it is vital to the life of the tree. Chlorophyll captures some of the sun's energy. The energy is used to combine water, which is taken up by the roots, and carbon dioxide, which is taken from the air, to produce simple sugars, the tree's food. The by-product of this process is oxygen.

During summer, chlorophyll is constantly breaking down and being replaced by the tree, which keeps the leaves green all season. As autumn approaches, the tree reacts to the reduced amount of daylight and starts to get ready for winter by shutting down the flow of nutrients to the leaves. Not only that, the leaves are starting to wear out from a season of hard work, making them ready to be shed.

At the leafstalk base (where the leaf attaches to the tree), a thin layer, called the abscission layer, starts to close off, reducing the flow of nutrients to the leaves. When this happens, chlorophyll production stops. Once chlorophyll is no longer the dominant compound in the leaves, other pigments, such as carotenoids, start to show. Carotenoids produce yellow, brown and orange colors and all the beautiful rustic shades in between.

Another group of pigment cells, called anthocyanins, begin to develop. Anthocyanins are not found in leaves during summer. These pigments, common in maple trees, give us the brilliant reds and purples of autumn. Unlike carotenoids, anthocyanins develop in sap during late summer and have a complex reaction inside the leaf when in the presence of bright sunlight and a chemical phosphate.

During summer, phosphates break down the sugars manufactured by chlorophyll. In autumn, the phosphate amount decreases and starts moving out of the leaves and into the tree. When this happens, the breakdown of sugar decreases. The brighter the light during this period, the greater the production of anthocyanins and the brighter red the leaves become.

If a tree is under drought stress or has poor health from a fungal or viral infection, the colors won't be as bright. Also, if the autumn season is dark and cloudy, the brightest colors won't develop. When the conditions of temperature, moisture and sunlight are all in the right amounts, we will enjoy a bright and colorful autumn.

Soon the abscission layer completely closes off, and the leaf dies and falls from the tree. The breakdown of dead leaves on the forest floor feeds nutrients back into the soil, where tree roots reabsorb them and help produce new leaves the following spring.

It's wonderful to think of all these chemical reactions taking place before your eyes when you stop and admire the blaze of autumn.

Critter Spots 'n Stripes

There are many strange animals, but the spotted skunk ranks up there near the top of the unique critter list. The Eastern Spotted Skunk (*Spilogale putorius*) is a very small black animal with many white marks or elongated spots running around its body, unlike the more familiar Striped Skunk

(*Mephitis mephitis*), which has only two white stripes running lengthwise down its body.

Spotted skunks weigh in at less than 2 pounds, with males slightly larger than females. They are about 18–20 inches long—but the tail takes up nearly half the length. Because of the diminutive size, when you first see one of these animals you are tempted to think it is a baby skunk.

All across the United States, all species of skunks are decreasing in population. In many areas they are locally extinct (extirpated). Loss of habitat and collisions with vehicles have helped contribute to their decline. Their defense—to stand and spray—is ineffective against speeding cars.

Like their striped cousin, spotted skunks are members of the weasel family. The Striped Skunk has a wide body and a full, bushy tail, while tiny spotted skunks have narrow bodies more like weasels and moderately furry tails. They also move more like weasels, with short, quick jumps and hops.

The Eastern Spotted Skunk, which is sometimes called Civet Cat, was once common in many parts of northern states. Populations peaked in the 1940s, but due to changes in agricultural practices, the population declined dramatically, with the biggest drop occurring over the past 20–30 years. Today this animal is rarely seen and has already been eliminated from many regions (extirpated). For this reason I feel it should be considered for official listing in many states.

Both species of skunks have the ability to spray an attacker 4–6 consecutive times with a bitter, foul-smelling mist from up to 15 feet away. So it's best to leave these animals alone. Both species smell the same.

Spotted skunks are true omnivores, feeding on mice, insects, small birds and their eggs, fruit, berries, fungi, frogs and salamanders. Compared with the Striped Skunk, spotted skunks are very secretive and rarely seen. In addition, the Striped Skunk rarely climbs trees, while the smaller spotted skunks make regular trips into trees in search of food and to escape predators such as foxes.

Mating occurs in February and March. Gestation is only 60 days, with mothers giving birth to 2–6 young. Babies are born in May and June and look like miniature adults. Early in winter, spotted skunks will start to den up and become inactive for several days—and even weeks at a time. However, they do not hibernate. They often come out during warm spells to search around for food.

So the next time you see a "baby" skunk in autumn, take a closer look. It just might be a Civet Cat.

Night Gliders

It was as dark as a night can be when I first heard the faint bird-like calls. They were coming from the top of a nearby tree. At first I wasn't sure what I was hearing. Songbirds are usually silent at night, and it was not an owl making this sound. After a moment I realized I was listening to the calls of a flying squirrel. Indeed, this was a special night.

There are only two species of flying squirrels—Northern Flying Squirrel and Southern Flying Squirrel. The Northern (*Glaucomys sabrinus*) inhabits coniferous forests across the northern portions of Minnesota, Wisconsin, Michigan and Pennsylvania. The Southern (*G. volans*) lives in deciduous forests just south of the Northern's range. Both of these squirrels are New World animals, which means they are found only in the Americas. That's not to say that Europe doesn't have any flying squirrels. They do—just not the species that occur here in North America.

Flying squirrels are the only nocturnal members of the squirrel family. But like many other animals, their common name doesn't describe them very accurately. Bats are the only mammals that can fly. Flying squirrels are not true flyers because they lack the ability to maintain or increase altitude while in the air. They are excellent at gliding, however, and can maneuver around objects during descent. Technically, they should be called gliding squirrels.

Northern Flying Squirrels are 7–9 inches long. Southern Flying Squirrels are smaller, only 5–6 inches. Both have a fluffy, flattened tail that is 3–6 inches long. The hairs on the tail extend out from the sides, giving it a flat shape and making it useful as a rudder or air brake.

Cute and fuzzy, they are covered with a very dense gray-to-brown fur that is incredibly soft. Like other squirrels, they have a white belly. However, the most notable aspect of these tiny gliders is their loose fold of skin, called the patagium, which stretches between the front and back legs to form a makeshift wing.

To become airborne, flying squirrels leap into the air, spread their legs and hold their tails straight out behind. The distance they can glide depends on the height at takeoff. The higher up they are when they jump, the farther they can glide. Most glides are 20–50 feet long.

Just before landing they use their tails as air brakes. They land facing up a tree trunk and immediately scramble to the far side, presumably to escape any flying predators, such as an owl, that might be in hot pursuit.

Flying squirrels are strictly nocturnal, which explains why we hardly see these gliding gurus. They have large eyes to help them see in the dark. Unlike other squirrels, flying squirrels rarely travel on the ground—so don't look for their tracks in the snow. However, like other squirrels they do eat seeds and nuts, but don't bury them in the ground. Instead, they cache extra nuts in holes and crevices in trees. They also eat fruit, fungi, tree buds, bird eggs and even baby birds. They are the most carnivorous of the squirrels, sometimes killing small birds or mice and occasionally eating dead flesh (carrion).

They remain active year-round, but live a short life of only 3–5 years. Mothers have 1–2 litters per year. Each litter consists of 3–5 young that are born blind, naked and helpless after a gestation of just 40 days.

Flying squirrels are gregarious animals, with many individuals living together. Their homes consist mainly of old woodpecker holes or abandoned gray squirrel nests. Sometimes they take up residence in birdhouses, Wood Duck boxes or occasionally in the attics of homes.

Fascinating Bats

It's funny. Just when we start to think about all the scary things that Halloween brings, such as bats, the bats are heading into hibernation. Halloween just wouldn't be the same without these furry, flying insect-eating critters.

Bats are fascinating animals. For one thing, they are the only mammals that fly. They are not birds or rats or mice. There are over 1,000 different kinds of bats in the world. That's an astonishing amount! In fact, bats make up one-quarter of all the world's mammals. Closer to home, we have 42 different kinds of bats in North America. All of the world's bats can be divided into two groups—fruit-eating and insect-eating bats.

Tree bats are solitary, unlike the social nature of cave bats. Just as their name implies, tree bats spend their days in the trees. Tree bats also migrate instead of retreating to caves each winter like the cave bats. The tree bats will migrate as far as the tropics of Central and South America.

Both tree and cave bats eat insects. On average, a single bat can eat 3,000–5,000 insects, including mosquitoes, per night. Multiply that times the number of bats in your neighborhood and you have some serious insect control going on. This is why it's become so popular to attract bats to your yard.

A common bat seen in backyards is the Little Brown Bat. The name accurately describes this species. During summer the female Little Browns come together in small maternal colonies, where they will give birth to single babies called pups. Females congregate in warm, out-of-the-way places such as hollow trees, rock crevices, bat houses or attics of homes. The males hang out by themselves.

Speaking of hanging, have you ever wondered why bats hang upside down? No one really knows where and when they started to do this, but there are a few theories. Bats that live in the colder northern climates need a sheltered place to hibernate. Caves are the perfect solution, but they have one major drawback. They usually don't have any convenient places to "sit." Hanging is the only alternative.

Bats don't have a problem hanging. Much like birds, bats have a locking tendon in their feet. When a bat hangs upside down, its body weight pulls on the tendon and locks the feet in a gripping position. That's why bats don't fall off a cave wall when they fall asleep.

Contrary to the old saying, bats are not blind. They have very good eyesight, probably as good as yours and mine. But good eyesight doesn't help in complete darkness. To offset this, bats have evolved a unique way to locate their prey in the dark—echolocation. It's a complicated process of sending out sound waves and waiting for the "echo" to come back. Based on this return sound, the bat can "see" in the dark. The echo-locating sound is beyond our hearing, so we can't hear this going on.

Bats also don't fly into your hair. Most people who claim to have witnessed this are misinterpreting the bat's actions. Flying insects are attracted to you and buzz around your head. The bats are after the insects and swoop down for an insect dinner. You only see the bat swooping for your head.

Another misinterpreted behavior concerns flying bats that are inside your house. Since bats are not really good flyers, they need to drop off their roost to gain airspeed before flying. When you approach a bat clinging to your wall, it will try to get away from you. It will drop off the wall to gain airspeed to fly away. It only appears to be swooping down to get you when it's only trying to get away.

Poorwill Peculiar

At the risk of sounding like a broken record, this column comes to you from the Arizona desert. During the day I'm working on locating and photographing several species of trees, cacti, wildflowers and small mammals—all for my series of field guides for Arizona. At night I have some time to explore the desert. In fact, if you ask me, nighttime is the best time to be out in the desert. All the desert critters become active at night.

One night just after dusk, I came across a very unusual bird—the Common Poorwill (*Phalaenoptilus nuttallii*). When I say it's unusual, I don't mean uncommon. I mean different from other birds. The poorwill occurs in the western half of the country, but because it is a nocturnal bird and one that is also very cryptic in color, it often goes unnoticed by the average person.

Even today, all nocturnal birds and animals are studied less than daytime (diurnal) species. Therefore, not much is known about these hidden critters.

The Common Poorwill is a resident of high, rolling prairies, desert scrub and rocky foothills at elevations around 4,000 feet. It is noted for its distinctive call and ability to enter a temporary daily hibernation called torpor. In fact, this is the only known bird to spend long periods during winter months completely inactive, day and night.

In 1946, a California ornithologist found a Common Poorwill in a rock crevice one day during winter. When he picked up the bird he could not detect a heartbeat or respiration, yet the bird was not dead. The temperature of this bird was 64–67 degrees—much lower than its normal temperature, which should be around 106 degrees. Over the next 88 days, during which the air temperatures remained around 40–42 degrees, the bird was examined, temperature and weight were monitored, and it was returned to the rock crevice. The temperature and weight of the bird remained the same, and after 12 weeks the bird woke up and flew off, just as air temperatures began to rise and its chief source of food—insects—became available. This was the first time that temporary hibernation (torpor) was reported in birds.

Since then we have learned a lot about the Common Poorwill. We now know that it becomes torpid when air temperatures range between 35–66 degrees, and that it uses only .35 ounce of stored fat over a 100-day period to keep alive. We have also discovered several other species of birds, such as Black-capped Chickadees, that use torpor to make it through cold temperatures. However, the poorwill is the only bird that uses torpor for extended periods of time, kind of like hibernation found in some large mammals. Recent studies show that poorwills in Arizona remain completely inactive on as many as 90 percent of all winter days and nights.

Poorwills are insect eaters that hunt from the ground or low perches at night just after the sun sets. They use the stars and moon, which help illuminate the night sky, to see flying insects in the darkness. They have extremely large eyes that allow them to see in the dark. When they see a large moth or beetle fly by, they quickly fly (sally) up to capture the insect before returning to the ground and waiting for another insect to pass by. They use very little energy to obtain their high-protein diet. They are such proficient hunters that they need to be active only for a couple hours after sunset to consume enough calories to last until the next night.

Back in the desert, I am driving down a dirt road just after sundown. The first poorwill illuminated in the headlights quickly flies off, as well as the second and third. However, the fourth one holds still. I am able to quietly exit the truck and sneak close enough to capture a couple images of this elusive night bird before it takes to the black sky and leaves me standing there in the glow of the headlights with the stars shining brightly above. Another great night in the desert.

Bird Flocks

As the old saying goes, "Birds of a feather flock together"—but have you ever stopped to think about why or how birds flock? The term "flocking" is generally used to describe many reasons why birds gather in large groups. For example, some birds, such as crows, gather in large groups to roost at night during winter. This is certainly considered a flocking behavior. Shorebirds gather in large groups along shorelines to feed. This is definitely flocking behavior. Also, many birds gather in large groups for migration. This is the kind of flocking behavior I want to discuss in this column.

Migrating in large numbers does have some major benefits when compared with migrating solo. For example, a large group of birds has more individuals to help see or locate food. During migration, birds encounter new areas where they've never been before and they need all the help they can get to find a plentiful food supply. More eyes mean more chances of finding suitable feeding stations.

Another benefit of migrating in large groups is safety in numbers. If you are a bird, the odds of getting eaten by a predator are greatly reduced if there are hundreds or thousands of others surrounding you. In addition, with all of your flockmates on the watch for a predator, you get the added benefit of an early warning system.

Traveling with others during migration also provides benefits for younger birds, who learn from the older or more experienced birds. It's helpful for locating safe places to stop while migrating and also for finding places to feed along the way. Of course, it is also very important when it comes to learning the route and final destination of the migration.

There are other advantages of migrating with a flock. Many waterfowl species, such as geese and swans, migrate in large groups. These groups are composed of several families or family groups with youngsters. When they are flying, they form various shaped formations. The most familiar is the V shape. While there is an ongoing debate about the benefits of flying in a V formation, several things can be assumed. For example, followers in a V formation probably derive an advantage of the rising and swirling air currents produced by the wing beats of the bird flying in front of them. This is called tip vortex and actually helps to keep the following bird aloft.

Models in controlled environments show that geese may save up to 20 percent of flight energy by flying in a V formation. Recently there was a study that attached heart rate monitors to free-flying geese. Heart rates in the birds that were not in the lead were lower than the heart rate of the bird in front, indicating that it took less physical strength to fly when in a V formation. This was a 10–20 percent savings in energy.

Some species, such as cormorants, fly in a straight line directly behind their flockmates. Similar to driving a car close behind another vehicle, the follower is drafting. Here is how this works. The vehicle in front continually displaces air when it's moving forward, creating a low-pressure area just behind the lead vehicle. Swirling air currents behind the lead vehicle can actually pull on a following vehicle, reducing the amount of energy it takes to maintain its speed. The same happens to birds flying in a straight line, thus reducing the amount of energy the birds need to migrate.

So it would seem there are some great benefits to being part of a flock. That's if you are a bird of a feather.

Feather Warming

November is upon us and with it comes the promise of snow and cold of the season. Brr . . . Time to pull out the old hat and gloves and relearn how to dress in layers. The next thing you know, long underwear will start to creep into our conversations and the weather will be the lead story on the evening news.

For the frigid days ahead, the kind of cold that makes even the most ardent nature lover cower, I prefer to wear my down-filled jacket. Thousands of tiny feathers provide me with the warmth needed to survive another cold day outdoors.

Feathers, just like the kind in my jacket, are key to a bird's survival. Feathers are what really make a bird a bird. No other animal has feathers. Feathers are made of a long, fibrous protein molecule known as keratin— the same substance that makes your hair.

A feather is composed of several parts. The shaft, or rachis, is the long, stiff part that runs up the center of a feather. Attached to the shaft are the vanes. Vanes are the soft part and make up the largest part of the feather, the color and the shape.

The vane is composed of small thread-like strands called barbs. Each barb has thousands of even smaller strands attached called barbules. The barbules are connected to barbicels with microscopic hooks called hamuli. Each strand is hooked to an opposing strand, much like the hooks of a zipper. If a twig or the wind disrupts a feather, simply zipping the affected area back together with a stroke of the bird's bill repairs it. This process is called preening.

Birds have six different types of feathers. Contour feathers cover a bird's body and are the largest feathers. These feathers give a bird its general shape and color and enable it to fly. Tail and wing feathers are examples of contour feathers. Contour feathers are equivalent to a bird's winter jacket.

Filoplumes are feathers that lay along the underside of contour feathers. They are hair-like feathers with just a few barbs on the end of a long thin shaft. They kind of look like miniature feather dusters.

Under the contour feathers and filoplumes are semiplumes—feathers that look like miniature contour feathers. Semiplumes look like messy contour feathers, only smaller, softer and fluffier. Under the semiplumes are down feathers. Down feathers appear furry with weak shafts and no vanes. Semiplumes and down feathers are for warmth and are equivalent to a bird's long underwear.

Some birds, such as woodpeckers, have special feathers, called bristles, around the eyes and nostrils. These hair-like feathers protect woodpeckers from sawdust while excavating holes in trees and can act like cat whiskers.

Powder down are feathers so soft and fragile that they crumble into powdery dust when touched. They are located usually on a bird's chest or near the tail. Pigeons, hawks, herons and other birds use powder down to help waterproof and condition their feathers by smearing the powder throughout their feathers.

Feathers are critical to keeping a bird warm. The more feathers, the warmer the bird stays. The Emperor Penguin of chilly Antarctica holds the record for the most feathers on a bird, with about 30,000 feathers. Large birds, such as swans, are a close second, at 25,000 feathers. Tiny warm-weather birds, such as hummingbirds, have only about 1,000 feathers.

Feathers are also what make a cardinal red and a jay blue. But it's not as simple as that. There are two ways color is produced in bird feathers: pigment and structural. Pigment embedded within a goldfinch's feather produces the bright yellow color. If you were to grind up a goldfinch feather, you would see a pile of yellow powder. The blue of Blue Jays and any other blue bird is created by absorbing some spectrum of the light and bouncing the rest (blue color) off a thin layer of cells on the feather's surface. That color is structurally produced. If you hold a Blue Jay feather up so light shines through it, you'll see its true color—grayish brown.

On a brisk fall day when you're bundled up in your warm down coat, you can thank our fine feathered friends for the warmth they provide.

Turkey, Chicken or Goose?

I am writing this just after eating Thanksgiving dinner
with my family and I am wondering just how many people
have given any thought to the turkey they just ate. What I
mean is, does anyone think about why there is white meat
and dark meat in a turkey?

It's all a matter of muscle and fibers. When we eat a
turkey, or chicken for that matter, we are eating the bird's
muscles and fibers. Different muscles do different jobs such as
walking and flying. Since turkeys are mainly ground-dwelling
birds, they spend a lot of time walking. They need large, strong leg
muscles that won't fatigue quickly and will be able to carry their heavy
body weight over long distances and for an extended period of time.
So the muscles in the legs contain a lot of red fibers (dark meat) that are
efficient at aerobic metabolism (requiring a lot of oxygen to get some
work done). Dark meat muscles are high in fat and sugar, which are fuel
for the muscles when the bird is walking or running.

Small songbirds that migrate long distances, such as orioles and tana-
gers, have mainly red fiber muscle (dark meat). These muscles sustain long
periods of activity using the stored fats and sugars to fly great distances.

Since turkeys spend most of their time on the ground walking and
sometimes running at high rates of speed to escape predators, they have
a lot of well-developed, tasty dark meat not only in their legs, but also in
the muscles that support the legs. Dark meat is my personal favorite.

White meat is a different story. The large breast muscles in turkeys
and chickens are white meat. This muscle is made up of fibers that are
light in color. Breast muscle is used only for flight.

Contrary to what many think, turkeys and chickens can fly short
distances. Turkeys have been clocked at up to 55 miles per hour in flight.

These birds are adapted for powerful short-distance flight that is used to escape predators. They literally burst into a very powerful flight from a standing position, but fatigue quickly and must glide to a stop and rest.

White meat breast muscle operates on anaerobic metabolism (operating without the need for oxygen). White meat doesn't have as much fat and sugar stored and so it looks, acts and, of course, tastes different.

Ducks and geese are long distance fliers, which means their breast meat consists of dark meat that is very high in fat and sugar content. So basically the birds with the most sustained flight have the darkest breast meat. In fact, hummingbirds have some of the darkest of breast meat.

Just a few things to think about the next time you are enjoying a meal of turkey or chicken.

Opossums

One animal goes beyond interesting and is downright unique—the opossum. Officially called the Virginia Opossum (*Didelphis virginiana*), it is traditionally an animal of the eastern and southern United States. This fascinating critter is expanding northward all across its range. It's not known why, but one could postulate that global warming is responsible.

Opossums are North America's only marsupial. Most people know that kangaroos are marsupials, but what does it mean to be a marsupial? It means that the babies have a very short gestation in the mother's womb (for example, 12–13 days for opossums) and spend the rest of the time in the mother's external fur-lined pouch.

The opossum has many other unique features that make it worth taking a closer look. An adult opossum is about the size of a small house cat, about 4–8 pounds. Opossums appear to be gray in color, but on closer inspection you will see that they're really like zebras minus the stripes—

black and white. The thick underfur is white with long black guard hairs dispersed throughout, giving the overall appearance of being gray.

The shorter underfur is primarily for warmth. Guard hairs are thicker and stiffer and do just what their name implies—they protect or guard the soft underfur and give an added measure of insulation and coloring.

The opossum has a long, narrow snout and a wide, gaping mouth, which allows room for a lot of teeth. In fact, opossums have more teeth than any other land mammal—50 teeth. They are true omnivores, which means they will eat both plants and animals. They have no specialized grinding molar teeth, like deer, nor do they have sharp cutting teeth, like beavers. All of their teeth are short and pointy.

During summer opossums eat insects, frogs, bird eggs, dead animals, berries, green plants and fruit. Winter is another story. They often eat road-killed animals, such as rabbits and raccoons, but this roadside feeding often leads them to become casualties. They also feed on sunflower seeds from backyard bird feeders.

Opossums have a long, naked, semiprehensile pinkish tail. Semiprehensile means the opossum can use its tail for holding on to branches for balance. The tail is usually not strong enough to hang from or use to swing like a monkey.

In northern tier states, having a naked tail is not a great idea. Often the tips of their tails turn black from frostbite. Their short naked ears are also subjected to the same cold treatment.

The feet of opossum are also very unique. Each foot has five toes. This is unlike many animals, which often have only four. Opossums also have an opposable big toe that resembles a thumb and is clawless. Every time I see an opossum track in the mud or snow it reminds me of a tiny handprint.

If you don't see many of these critters, it might be because they are nocturnal. Active mostly at night, they are non-sociable. Males and females get together only to breed. The mother is limited to 14 young annually because that's the number of nipples available.

After birth, the young, who are blind, naked and only the size of a lima bean, about ¼ inch long, climb unaided through the mother's fur until they reach the safety of her pouch. The young will spend the next two months attached to one of the mother's nipples, growing quickly.

After emerging from the pouch, the young will ride on their mother's back by clinging to her fur using their opposable thumbs. How about that for being nuisance children?

Wildcat Country

There are many magnificent animals in the world, but very few are as remarkable as the Cougar (*Puma concolor*). Also called Mountain Lion, Panther, Catamount or Puma, the cougar is a member of the feline family (Felidae). I have much respect and admiration for these big cats. They are secretive, usually solitary, animals that were once found widespread on all continents except Antarctica and Australia. They are probably one of the most difficult animals to see or photograph in the wild.

The cougar is one of the few large cat species that doesn't have a spotted coat. It is a uniform light brown, with a white chest and belly. Its fur is short, but extremely thick and a very good insulator. A large round head, short ears and a long rope-like tail with a dark tip are characteristic features of this proficient carnivore.

An adult cougar is four times larger than the more common bobcat, which is slightly larger than a house cat.

The average adult cougar can weigh over 100 pounds, with males weighing slightly more than females. They are solitary animals except for mating, which is usually only every other year for adult females.

After mating at any time of year, a mother will give birth to a litter of 2–3 kittens with dark spotted fur. Kittens will nurse for up to six weeks and stay with their mother for up to two years, learning how and what to hunt. The kittens will lose their spots at about six months of age.

Proficient hunters, cougars hunt during the night or day, concentrating mostly on large mammals, such as White-tailed Deer, but will take just about any mammal they can catch. In general, they take only old or crippled deer. They are not long-distance runners, so they rely on stealth, stalking and then springing or pouncing on their prey, often from a tree or other elevated surface.

It is believed that the cougar was the most widespread mammal in the New World when Europeans first came to the Americas. It ranged throughout all of North, Central and South America. Unlike many animals, it adapted well to many different environments, from deep forests to windswept prairies, snowy mountains and arid deserts. Today most cougars are confined to the mountains of western states and Canada, but they are popping up all over their range.

Individual cougars can range over hundreds of miles in search of food or a mate. Males tend to roam farther than females. Many reported cougar sightings are formerly captive animals that escaped from their owners or were turned loose by errant owners who had the mistaken belief that a cougar would somehow make a good pet. Nothing could be further from the truth. A large, powerful animal with the skills of a cougar cannot and will not be a good pet. Anyone with such a notion should reconsider his or her choice.

Winter

Antler Ornament

Now is a time when many of us turn our attention to White-tailed Deer. Mankind has a long history of association with deer. We have depended on its meat for food, its skin for clothing and its antlers for tools and decoration for thousands of years.

A deer's antlers seem to hold great attraction for people. But like many things in nature that we covet, there is also a lot of confusion about antlers. For instance, many don't know the difference between antlers and horns. Horns are permanent and are retained for the life of the animal. They are made of keratin with a bony core. Keratin is a protein substance without a blood supply. Hooves, hair, claws and nails, for example, are composed of keratin. Horns are found on mammals such as American Bison and Bighorn Sheep. They tend to be relatively short and thick.

The Pronghorn, sometimes called antelope, is unique to North America. It is an exception to the horn/antler rules because its horns have a bony core with an outer horn sheath, which is shed each year. Pronghorn horns are like a combination of horns and antlers. Both males and females have horns, but the males' horns are much larger.

Antlers are completely different from horns. Antlers are made of solid bone. Only members of the deer family, Cervidae, such as deer, elk and moose, grow antlers. Except for caribou and reindeer, only the males have antlers, with the odd exception of a rare female with a hormonal imbalance, which sometimes grows a set of small antlers. Antlers are the fastest growing bones in the natural world, and, depending on the species, can grow as large as 4–5 feet long and weigh several pounds.

All antlers start from a small swelling on a male deer's head called a pedicel or antler bud. These first appear as a tiny twist of hairs on a young male fawn's head and are visible from nearly the time of birth. It is the pedicel that is the key to a large antler. For example, young male deer

with poor nutrition or deficient in testosterone develop small
pedicels and thus small antlers.

I think most people would agree that the size of a deer's
antlers is dependent upon age, nutrition and inherited traits.

But there is not agreement about the
degree to which each factor plays in
the eventual size of the antlers.

Antlers start to grow in early spring. The
length of daylight triggers the growth. From the
beginning, the newly growing antlers are covered with a
network of blood vessels and nerve endings known as "velvet" because it
looks and feels like velvet or suede.

The rapidly growing antlers receive blood through the outer velvety
skin and also through an inner core vessel. The velvet is very fragile and
tender. It bruises easily and bleeds if it is damaged and even suffers frostbite if frozen. So a buck must remain careful during the growth period.
This means no sparring with other bucks or running into tree branches.
If an antler is seriously injured during growth, it will be deformed at
the place of injury. What is really amazing is that the antlers will also
"remember" an injury, and succeeding antlers will also be deformed as
long as the buck lives.

As amazing as antlers are, what is more incredible is how antlers
grow. Researchers have proven that a buck must borrow large amounts
of calcium, the chief component of antlers, from the body. The place
where this calcium comes from is the ribs and sternum. So much calcium
is taken from the ribs that they become very brittle and often break during
the critical period of antler growth. However, the research also shows that
a healthy buck takes this in stride and fractures heal smoothly and with
minimal discomfort.

Antlers are the fastest growing bones in the mammalian world. In
fact, the mobilization of minerals from a White-tail's skeleton to its antlers
is so remarkable that it may someday give us insight into the mysteries of

osteosarcoma (bone cancer) and also osteoporosis (a serious bone disease of older women). There is much to learn from the natural world around us.

I am always amazed at the different colors of antlers. They can range from ivory to dark mahogany. The coloration is due to staining from rubbing the antlers on tree bark or from blood hemoglobin when the antler is still in velvet. I have also seen antlers with different colored mosses and lichens growing on them, particularly at the base, which makes the antlers appear to be different colors.

By the end of the mating season, a buck's antlers can be nearly white. Rain and sun do much to bleach antlers. By the end of January and occasionally February, bucks will shed or discard their antlers. Casting or shedding of the antlers occurs with little to no pain and very little blood. In fact, the attachment spot heals quickly, usually within a couple days, and new antlers start to grow within weeks, starting the process all over again.

Nothing goes to waste in nature, and discarded antlers just don't lie around the forest floor forever. They are chewed by a host of small mammals, presumably to gain the calcium. In fact, a friend of mine once drilled a hole through a deer antler and threaded a heavy gauge wire through it. Then he secured the antler to the ground with the wire and noted how long it took for the antler to be eaten. In a short eight weeks, there wasn't much left of the antler.

As incredible as antlers are, what is even more amazing is why a deer has antlers in the first place. Think about it. Of what use are a buck's antlers? If you examine a buck's entire year, you will find that antlers are more of a hindrance than a help. From the day the antlers start to grow, a deer must take great care to not injure the delicate growing antlers. During spring and summer, bucks act and move around like does rather than the usual wild-eyed bucks. At this time, any disagreements between bucks are handled doe-like, with much rearing on hind legs and flailing with their forefeet because they need to protect their growing antlers.

During summer it is the females that are dominant, not the bucks. In fact, there is good evidence that bucks live in summertime bachelor groups because the does have driven them into segregation. So why do bucks have antlers?

A common theory is that bucks grow antlers to defend against natural enemies and other bucks. But if that were true, why don't female White-tails have antlers as well? Does are preyed on even more than the bucks. Also, why don't the bucks retain their antlers (more horn-like) throughout winter, when predation is the worst? Besides, isn't the best defense of a White-tail its ability to quickly run away? Every deer I have come across has responded to me by running away, not standing and fighting.

An intriguing theory as to why bucks have antlers suggests that antlers are for attracting mates—to impress the girls. Antlers for deer are kind of like fancy cars and nice clothing for people. It is widely accepted that a male cardinal's bright colors are a signal to potential mates that he is a healthy male with a good territory, and that he has a good food supply available to him. Food is the sole component needed for brightly colored feathers. Female birds choose their mates based on how the male looks and how well he sings. Since deer don't sing, it would appear that does look for bucks with the largest antlers for a mate. Therefore, large antlers are indicative of his good health, food supply and genetics.

Earlier we talked about how a buck's diet is a major factor in the growth of antlers. The more nutritious the diet, the larger and thicker the antlers will grow. That, along with good genetics, will produce bucks with an impressive rack.

Not only do large antlers impress the girls, the size of a buck's antlers establishes a place or ranking in White-tail hierarchy. Early in the season, bucks with the most massive antlers and swollen necks will spar with bucks that are approximately their own size to determine domi-nance. The smaller, less dominant bucks rarely challenge the large bucks. Once the strongest and most skilled buck establishes its ranking, the males usually don't have to fight again and all of their attention is focused on breeding. Really, a White-tailed Deer's antlers are a visible way to say, "Hey, I am a strong and healthy male that will produce strong and healthy offspring—so consider me for breeding."

This brings me to a photography trip where I spent several days with a moose researcher in Canada's Riding Mountain National Park in Manitoba. Researcher Vince Crichton, whom you may have seen on an Animal Planet Channel special, uses a stuffed moose head with interchangeable antlers to interact with bull moose and observe their behavior. He would strap the moose head to his chest, kind of like a reverse backpack, and using a moose call, would walk up to bull moose during the rut. The goal was to observe the reaction that the bull moose would have to Vince's antlers.

Vince has established that when he approached a moose with smaller antlers, presumably a less dominant moose, that moose would not challenge Vince and his large antlers. Bulls with equal or larger antlers would stand their ground and become agitated, indicating their willingness to fight by rocking their heads back and forth to show off their antlers.

For several days I followed Vince around the north woods of Riding Mountain National Park and observed the behavior of the moose. I was amazed at how those bull moose didn't see a man with a moose head strapped to his chest. They seemed to see only the antlers, further indicating how important antlers are to members of the deer family.

Albino White-tails

I rolled out of bed at 4 a.m. muttering unpleasantries under my breath about getting out of a nice warm bed on a very cold winter morning. But getting up early and venturing out into the bone-crunching cold is part of the job for this wildlife photographer.

Three layers of clothing, extreme weather boots and my warmest hat and gloves and I am all set to go. I made sure my camera batteries were fully charged the night before. Camera memory cards were in my pocket and my GPS was fired up. I was ready.

I drove about three hours one way to search for a very special critter. For the past four years I have been traveling to this region to photograph a unique animal. So, what is this special critter that beckons me out of bed? A pure white White-tailed Deer (*Odocoileus virginianus*).

All across this great nation there are pockets of these white ghosts roaming the forests. Estimates are about one in every 30,000 deer is white. I have read other estimates that one in every 100,000 is white. Of course, there is no way to confirm that, but I am comfortable in saying that white deer are not very common at all.

Which brings me to the sticky subjects of why these deer are white, and what do you call them? Most people would call them albino. Albinism is a condition in which the body cannot produce the pigments needed to color hair and skin. It is caused by a recessive gene. In order for albinism to occur, it requires both parents to carry the recessive gene and pass it on to the young.

By definition, albinism is the complete absence of normal pigmenta- tion. This means no pigment at all and results in an animal, such as a deer, having pink eyes, nose, ears and hooves. The lack of pigment in the irises of the eyes reduces the animal's ability to see. Combined with a white coat that makes the animal stand out like a snowball on a summer's day, this means these critters don't last very long in the predator and prey world of nature. In fact, most albino animals don't live very long and rarely live long enough to reproduce.

So how does that explain the pockets of white deer in the woods? I suspect it's because the deer are not true albino, but rather a partial or imperfect albino. The white deer I am photographing don't have pink eyes, but rather gray to almost blue eyes. Apparently they have a small amount of pigment in their eyes, giving them relatively normal eyesight and thus the ability to survive and reproduce.

Some deer are white with patches of brown, giving them the appearance of being spotted or looking like a pinto horse. These are called piebald deer. Piebald deer are thought to be slightly more common and presumably live longer and reproduce more often than albino deer. The same genetic deficiency causes piebald deer and albino deer.

I have always enjoyed photographing the oddities of nature, and these white deer are some of my favorites.

Key Deer at the Keys

In commemoration of the passage of the Endangered Species Act (December 1973), let's take a look at an animal that has directly benefited from this important legislation—the Key Deer.

The Key Deer (*Odocoileus virginianus clavium*) is a subspecies of the familiar White-tailed Deer (*O. virginianus*). It is one of 28 subspecies of deer and is the smallest race of deer in North America. An average adult stands 2 feet tall at the shoulders. Bucks (males) average 80 pounds and does (females) average 65 pounds. In all other respects, these deer appear just like the deer that visit your backyard, only much smaller.

Key Deer occur only on a few select islands or "keys" located in southern Florida. They require Pine Rockland habitat, which is composed of several pine tree species on what tends to be the highest elevation (several feet above sea level) of each island. Fresh water seems to be the factor limiting where the deer thrive. After heavy rains, depressions in the ground collect the fresh rainwater, which is critical to the deer's survival.

I met with Shane Whisenant, the Key Deer biologist at the National Key Deer Refuge on Big Pine Key, Florida. Shane is a man with a passion for the Key Deer. He explained to me that the refuge was established in 1957 when it was discovered that the total population of Key Deer had fallen to about 27 animals.

Unlimited hunting and habitat destruction were presumably the factors leading to the decline of this tiny deer.

Today, more than 50 years later, the Key Deer is on the rebound, thanks to specific habitat management such as prescribed burns to open the forest. These efforts provide a source of native grasses for the deer to feed on and the restoration of freshwater pools.

The biology of the Key Deer is similar to that of its larger counterpart in the Midwest. Life span is approximately 7–8 years, with most females breeding at 1–2 years of age. Bucks don't start mating until they are slightly older and have developed large antlers, enabling them to compete against other bucks. The rut takes place in September through November. Gestation is about seven months, with most does giving birth to twins in April or May.

Hunting of Key Deer is prohibited. However, about 100–150 deer are killed each year. Most deaths result from hits by cars or encounters with domestic dogs. In 2003, 137 deer were lost—91 of them to automobile collisions. Both of these causes of mortality are something the staff at the National Key Deer Refuge is actively working to reduce.

Do yourself a favor. Next time you are visiting southern Florida, make a trip to Big Pine Key (part of the chain of islands known as the Florida Keys) to see these wonderful animals. They come out along the roadsides late in the day and can be observed from your car. Please don't attempt to feed or touch the deer. This only encourages the deer to come closer to the roads. And the last thing they need is to be closer to a collision with a car.

Animal Tracking Art

A light dusting of snow and cold temperatures create the perfect conditions for one of my favorite wintertime nature activities—tracking. Animal tracking is an ancient art going back thousands of years. This skill was absolutely essential for the survival of the early hunter-gatherers.

Today's naturalists find animal tracking a great excuse to get out and enjoy winter. It is a fun and easy activity the whole family will like. Children are intrigued with each individual track, and adults like the challenge of identifying what made the track.

Long trips in the car are not necessary to find animal tracks. You can start in your own backyard. Rabbits and squirrels are so abundant that you and your family can learn how to tell them apart in just a few minutes. Best of all, you don't need any special equipment or training—just the time and desire to get out and have some fun.

Chances are you won't see a fox or raccoon on your next walk, but finding their tracks is easy. Some of the possible tracks you are likely to see on your animal tracking adventure (depending on where you are) are deer, squirrels, skunks, foxes, raccoons, rabbits, coyotes and a wide variety of songbirds.

The best way to start tracking is to watch the rabbits and squirrels in your own backyard. Watch how their paws land and observe if they hop or walk. Next, go outside right after they make some tracks and take a good look. I often find that sketching the pattern of tracks on a notebook helps me remember what made which track. And you can start your own tracking journal.

When examining tracks, first look at one individual track and then at the pattern of several tracks together. When looking at a single track, note the general shape to determine if there is a heel pad and, if so, what it looks like. Look for any toe and claw marks. This will help you determine the direction of travel. Count the toes and determine whether they are all on the same side of the track. Birds have four toes—three forward and one hind.

After examining one track, look at a group of tracks to see the pattern of the animal's movement. Groups of tracks are defined by how each track falls in sequence. When the hind track of an animal falls into the front print, it is called direct registration. Foxes use this method of walking. It is essential for walking without making a sound. A fox is able to see where it is placing its front paw and choosing a step without snapping a twig or rustling leaves. The hind foot lands in the same chosen silent spot of the front paw. A fox's track looks like a straight line of single tracks.

Indirect registration is when the hind track falls just outside of the front track. Tracks made by your family dog are a good example of this. Years of domestication have made our canine pets "sloppy" when they walk. They have lost their ability to walk silently.

Tracks like those made by raccoons will have alternating hind and front tracks, called an alternating pattern. Bounding and hopping describe a complete set of four tracks. Squirrels and rabbits leave these kinds of tracks. Walking animals, such as opossums and raccoons, leave a continuous line of alternating tracks. Tracks that look like tiny human hands seen along a creek usually belong to a raccoon or opossum.

Otter tracks combine paw prints and belly slides—long, wide drag marks left in snow as otters slide on their bellies.

Note your surroundings and look for other clues. If you are in the woods and see hopping tracks that start and stop at a tree, they most likely belong to a squirrel. Birds often leave some of the most interesting tracks. Look for associated wing and tail marks left in the snow by an errant wing or tail. Opossum and mice drag their tails and leave a characteristic mark in the snow along with regular track marks.

Animal tracking is all about having fun and getting outside with your family.

Christmas Evergreens

When Christmas is just around the corner, many of us are searching for a perfect Christmas tree. One not too tall, one with no bare spots, and most importantly—one that won't drop all its needles the minute after you've finished decorating it.

The Christmas tree is a huge part of our American Christmas tradition, but why? There are many different stories about the origins, but most agree it started with the Germans. The evergreen nature of the tree was a symbol of life during the depths of winter, when everything else was brown and dead. It brought hope and reassurance when times were tough.

Today we go to Christmas tree lots overflowing with a wide assortment of trees—pine, spruce and fir. But how do you know which one is which? Here are a few tips to help identify your green Christmas beauty.

First, look at the leaves. That's right—the leaves! Pine needles are just a type of leaf and, like all trees, the leaves of evergreens (needles) are different on each species of tree. Next, count the number of needles growing in each group. Each group, called a bundle, originates from a small brown papery sheath. A bundle can have one to five needles growing together.

If your tree has two or more needles in a bundle, then you have one of the true pine trees. One of the more popular Christmas pines is the Scotch pine. It has two long needles bundled together at the base. Each needle is twisted, which gives the tree a fuller look. Also very popular is the white pine. It has bundles of five long needles. Each of these needles is several inches long and very straight. When you run your hands over a white pine, it feels soft and velvety.

If your tree has only one needle per bundle, you have one of the very popular spruce or fir trees. It's easy to distinguish between these two types of evergreens. Try shaking hands with your tree. If the needles are very sharp, you probably have a spruce. Spruce trees have square, four-sided needles, so another way to check is to pull off a single needle and roll it between your fingers. If you have trouble feeling the edges, cut the needle in cross section so you can see its square shape. A handy way to remember how to identify a spruce tree is with an "S"—for "spruce" and "square."

If your needles are flat or blunt, you have a fir tree. Shaking hands with a fir tree doesn't result in a trip to the emergency room like it would with a spruce, because fir needles are soft and pliable. Pull off one and take a closer look at the flat shape. A good way to remember how to identify a fir tree is with an "F"—for "fir" and "flat."

So to recap, if you have a tree with two or more needles in a bundle, you have a pine. Square single needles are spruce, and flat single needles are fir. Easy!

Merry Christmas!

Dead Tree Havens

A friend once reminded me of something very valuable that I take for granted, because it makes complete sense to me. However, the message hasn't reached most of the general public—the value of dead trees!

I think it is safe to say that we can all appreciate the value of a living tree. Living trees bring value in many ways, both seen and unseen. Land developers know that land with a stand of healthy trees is worth more than land devoid of trees. Homeowners know that trees have value in the form of aesthetics—they just look good. Trees also provide much-needed cool shade during hot summers. Conversely, trees help to block the biting wind of winter. It is safe to say that live trees are universally accepted as a good thing.

So, how about dead trees? How does your perception of value change? For me, it doesn't. Dead or dying trees, called snags, are extremely valuable, provided they are not in danger of falling and injuring someone or damaging property. Dead trees supply the same (and in some instances, more) food, shelter and nesting sites for wildlife as do live trees.

Woodpeckers usually don't excavate cavities in healthy live trees. The outer bark and inner wood is often too hard to excavate a home. The softer wood of a dead tree is ideal for birds, such as Red-bellied Woodpeckers, Northern Flickers, Downy Woodpeckers and Black-capped Chickadees, to excavate their nest cavities. Chalk one up for dead trees.

Dead trees house thousands of insects. Several species of bark beetles bore easily into dead trees, creating amazing patterns just under the bark. Carpenter ants build large nests with thousands of individuals in just one dead tree.

While dead trees are great places to build homes, they are also great places to find something to eat. Fast and ferocious centipedes hunt within cavities of dead trees. The centipede's large jaw-like claws carry a poison that paralyzes their victims, but is harmless to humans. The multitude of insects living in a dead tree is a regular smorgasbord to centipedes and also to many insect-eating birds, such as woodpeckers, nuthatches and chickadees, not to mention furry critters that eat insects such as raccoons, skunks and opossums.

Dead trees are also filled with a wide variety of fungi. The hyphal threads of the fungus penetrate through the tree, softening the tough cells called lignin. The fungal work starts the process of recycling the nutrients locked in the tree back into the soil. Without fungi, every tree that died and fell in the forest would take hundreds of years to break down.

According to studies conducted by the U.S. Forest Service, as many as 85 species of birds used dead trees for nesting or as an all-you-can-eat salad bar—only the salad bar would be stocked with insects.

Some birds, such as Brown Creepers and several warbler species, build their nests behind the sloughing bark of dead trees and nowhere else.

Snags also provide a lofty perch with unobstructed views for birds of prey, such as owls and hawks, to hunt for woodland mice, moles and shrews. Several species of flycatchers (small woodland birds) perch on dead tree branches, waiting for a passing insect to eat for lunch.

If a standing dead tree provides a virtual megamall of opportunities, than a brush pile is a wildlife heaven. A brush pile is a simple pile of tree branches placed in an out-of-the-way part of your yard. Many small animals, such as chipmunks and rabbits, and a wide variety of birds utilize brush piles for shelter, to escape from predators or for a place to rest and take a quick midday nap.

Overwintering butterflies, along with several species of reptiles and amphibians, also use backyard brush piles for shelter. Brush piles can mean the difference between life and death for some birds during extreme cold snaps in winter.

Just think . . . all you have to do is leave a few dead trees standing or create a small brush pile in your backyard, and you could be providing a comfortable home complete with a stocked refrigerator for your favorite birds and animals.

Surviving Winter

Peering into the steel blue stillness of a midwinter evening, I am struck by the profound coldness. When the temperatures plummet to near zero, my mind turns to the amazing ways that animals and birds cope with such extreme weather.

Winter poses several challenges to wildlife. Scarce food supplies and limited water are just a few obvious challenges to winter survival. Extremely cold temperatures, strong winds, driving snow and nights that seem to go on forever can be deadly for birds. Each winter we lose many of our birds to the rigors of winter weather. It's how nature works—the survival of the fittest.

Birds have many adaptations to survive winter weather. Wintering birds, such as the American Goldfinch and Black-capped Chickadee, add additional feathers in preparation for winter. The typical goldfinch or chickadee is covered with about 1,000 feathers during summer and more than 2,000 in winter. During very cold days and nights, birds fluff up their feathers, reducing the amount of heat loss by up to 30 percent. However, extra feathers alone are not enough to make it through a winter night.

Birds have a unique circulatory system in their legs to help them cope with cold temperatures. Warm arterial blood from the interior of the bird on its way to the feet passes through a network of small passages that run alongside the cold-returning blood from the feet. The network of vessels acts like a radiator and exchanges the heat from the outgoing arterial blood to the cold venous blood. This system ensures that no heat is lost and the bird's feet receive a constant supply of life-sustaining blood. That's also why ducks can swim in freezing water and not get cold.

Fat is another important winter weather survival adaptation. Fat acts as an insulator in addition to a food reserve. During the day, birds eat to build up fat reserves. On average, a bird can put on up to 15 percent of its body weight in extra fat before it has trouble flying.

Birds don't have brown fat—the kind you and I have. Instead, they have white fat. White fat is a high-energy fuel used to power the bird's warming process, which is called thermogenesis. Thermogenesis is just a fancy name for shivering. All birds from crows to chickadees continually shiver during winter to maintain their core body temperature at about 106–109 degrees, depending on the species. That is an amazingly high temperature when compared with the surrounding air temperature. Only a thin layer of feathers separates what could be a temperature difference of more than a hundred degrees.

Shivering produces heat five times the normal basal rate and can maintain a normal body temperature for 6–8 hours at 70 degrees below zero. Without shivering, the bird's body temperature would drop and the bird would die.

At night, chickadees and other birds take shivering (or I should say the lack of shivering) one step further. To conserve heat, chickadees can lower their body temperature by stopping their shivering. These periods of inactivity allow the bird's body temperature to slowly cool until it drops about 10–12 degrees. At this point the bird enters a state of unconsciousness called torpor.

Nearing morning, the periods of inactivity decrease until the bird is constantly shivering again and the body core temperature is back in the normal range, which is when the bird regains consciousness. The result of this controlled hypothermia is an energy savings of up to 20 percent during a typical winter night. Energy conservation is very important when you consider how little fat a bird can store.

Based on a daily increase of body fat (15 percent), a bird has about 16–24 hours of energy reserves to carry it through a typical winter night. That is why it is imperative that a bird gets out early in the morning and finds food regardless of the weather. Have you ever seen a chickadee or junco flitting around your feeder in the middle of a blizzard? If it doesn't replenish its fat reserves, the bird will not make it through the next night.

You can help our bird friends survive another cold winter simply by filling your feeder with some black-oil sunflower seeds.

Red-headed Woodpecker

The temperature was hovering just below freezing and I was going on my sixth hour of sitting in my 4-foot by 4-foot nylon blind, waiting. This is when this job gets a little mind-numbing. I was waiting to photograph an elusive bird when I realized a question kept running through my head over and over—when is a woodpecker not a woodpecker? I answered myself—when it is a Red-headed Woodpecker.

As far as a species goes, I think the Red-headed Woodpecker is a woodpecker most unlike other woodpeckers. Let me explain.

Lately I have been concentrating my photographic efforts on a specific species—the Red-headed Woodpecker (*Melanerpes erythrocephalus*). This means I spend day after day sitting in my blind, watching and waiting for the woodpeckers to come close enough to photograph. It allows me endless hours to watch their every movement and interaction. At night I spend time researching and reading what others have observed about the species. I also read all the research papers that have been published about the species. The next day I go back and sit and watch and wait some more. (One interesting note is that this species is one of the least-studied woodpeckers in North America.)

I find several things most intriguing. When compared with other species of woodpeckers, the Red-headed Woodpecker is very unique. For example, one of the first things I noticed is when a Red-head lands on a small branch or twig, it lands perpendicular to the branch. All other woodpeckers will land parallel to the branch. So in other words they perch more like a songbird than a woodpecker.

When feeding during winter, Red-heads prefer to feed on the ground, hopping around like robins. They are only one of three woodpecker species that feeds on the ground. During fall and winter they prefer nuts, such as acorns and hickory nuts, as their food source. In fact, they are dependent on this food so much that they gather large quantities of nuts and store them for later consumption. Red-headed Woodpeckers are only one of four species of woodpeckers that will store food for later consumption. Keep in mind there are nearly 200 woodpecker species in the world and only four of them store food. This is a very unusual behavior.

During summer the Red-heads change their diet mostly to flying insects. In much the same way that flycatchers (a group of birds) feed, a Red-headed Woodpecker will sit on a branch, perpendicular, and wait for a winged insect to fly by and then sally forth to grab its meal. Red-heads will also drop to the ground to grab grasshoppers and other large ground-dwelling insects. They are also one of the most omnivorous woodpeckers, eating the eggs of other birds, baby birds and even small mammals, such as mice, if they find them dead.

Unlike most woodpecker species, Red-headed Woodpeckers are monomorphic, which means the males and females look exactly the same. In fact, even researchers who have the birds in their hands can't tell them apart. This is one of the large stumbling blocks to studying this species. Nearly all other woodpeckers show some difference between the sexes.

The population of Red-headed Woodpeckers has fluctuated greatly over the past 200 years. Early European settlers in North America found this bird in great abundance. In the 1840s, John James Audubon wrote, "I would not recommend to anyone to trust their fruit to the Red-heads for they not only feed on all kinds as they ripen, but destroy an immense quantity besides." Starting in the early 1900s, the numbers of Red-heads started to drop dramatically. Estimates based on some bird surveys indicated more than a 50 percent drop in Red-headed Woodpecker populations over the past 100 years. At this rate of decrease we may be looking at the extinction of this stunning species in the next 50 years.

Owling Arizona

It was a warm and slightly breezy evening. Temperatures were hovering at a comfortable 65 degrees. Perfect for a night hike to search for owls in the desert mountains. The stars were blazing brightly above us, and I could see the winter constellation Orion reminding me that it was indeed wintertime. These clear warm nights are some of the best parts of owling in southeastern Arizona during winter.

I am in the company of "Owl Guy" Rick Bowers, who is by far one of the most experienced wildlife photographers and bird experts in southeastern Arizona. We are hiking down a narrow trail in the mountains with a bright moon to guide our way. We stop every so often to listen for the telltale call of the Whiskered Screech-Owl, a tiny owl of oak forests at elevations around 5,000 feet.

As we walk, I hear only the sound of our footsteps—no owls. Finally, we hear our tiny quarry about 12 feet up, near the top of an Alligator-bark Juniper tree. This evergreen species grows along the banks of streams that cascade down the mountains. We approach the owl and for the first time we switch on our oversized flashlight. There in the beam of the light is the elusive Whiskered Screech-Owl, calling from his perch. I quickly set up my camera and flash gear and attach it to my tripod. I peer through the camera lens and manually focus. My flash pops and lights up this section of the valley. A beautiful tiny owl in a wonderful mountain setting—what a sight! We turn off the flashlight and give each other high fives before heading down to our car.

Day two of owling is clear and warm and the sun is shining brightly. We drive out to a remote mountain valley where another special owl resides—the Spotted Owl (Mexican subspecies). The drive up the valley is bumpy, with several washes where water flows over the road. We park and gather our camera gear and some water for the long hike. The trail is a narrow path no wider than our footsteps and it follows a dry stream bed. We traverse over small and large boulders and use tree trunks as handholds to help pull us up. As usual, the camera gear is getting heavy. The elevation is slightly over 5,000 feet, temperatures have dipped into the 40s and the wind picks up as we climb higher.

We stop occasionally where the habitat looks good for owls. When we can get no higher, we fan out and start a tree-by-tree search. Within 10–15 minutes we find an owl not in a tree, but sitting on a rock of a steep-sided canyon wall, trying to stay out of the wind. We set up the camera gear once again and snap some great images. The owl hears something and flies off, but doesn't go far. We move down and take a few more pictures. After another high five, we get ready for the long hike back down the trail.

Day three finds us on the road again. This time we're going to hit several places in one day to photograph as many owls as possible. First stop is an abandoned, dilapidated bridge in the middle of the desert. Sheltered beneath are two sleeping Barn Owls. Very cool! Second stop is a wonderful desert inn that rents rooms to bird watchers. We amble over to the owner's large pole barn, where two adult Barn Owls are roosting in the rafters. Last, we drive to the final stop of the day, a wildlife management area. Nearing sunset, we hike with our cameras to a grove of trees where owls are known to roost. We find at least three Long-eared Owls, two Great Horned Owls and five or more Barn Owls.

As the sun sets, the Great Horns takes flight first and perches briefly on the roof of an old shed. Flying out to a grove of trees, he perches on a tall treetop and is silhouetted against the orange glow of the setting sun. Next, the Barn Owls give a few hoarse calls before taking flight. They fly in several tight circles before landing back in the trees. They do this a few times before taking off across the desert in search of a meal. Now the Long-eared Owls begin to stir. Suddenly they blast out of the thick vegetation and head out for a night of hunting.

It's been a successful day—three species of owls! We are dog-tired and head back for a couple hours of sleep before rising predawn for another day of photography.

For the next three days we head high into the Arizona mountains near the Mexican border for more Spotted Owls and Whiskered Screech-Owls. Each night we stand outside in the cool mountain air under a starry sky and listen for the calling of owls. Again we locate a Whiskered Screech-Owl and set out to capture another image of these elusive birds of the night. This continues for three more nights—until we are so exhausted that we head back to town. Overall, it's hard to beat this trip when it comes to owling in Arizona.

Yellowstone in Winter

Few places on this planet have more beauty and grandeur than our national park—Yellowstone. It's also one of the few places in North America that has an intact wildlife ecosystem, where all top predators and their prey interact in the daily struggles of life. The best time to witness this predator/prey relationship is in the dead of winter, when snow is deep, temperatures are bone-chilling cold and nights are long and dark.

I've come to Yellowstone countless times during summer, but this is my first winter visit. And I am not disappointed. For one week I have been fortunate enough to watch and photograph the daily lives of the animals that call this magnificent park home.

A typical day consists of rising at 5 a.m. and packing the camera gear and extra winter clothing. I'm on the road hours before sunrise to make the drive into the Lamar Valley. There's no time to eat breakfast, so a cold bagel while traveling is the morning routine.

On most mornings, the mountainous roads have a light coating of snow from the daily snow showers. At daybreak, the sun sheds light on the majestic snow-capped mountains that surround the valley. In the open meadows, herds of elk and bison are bedded down in deep snow, chewing their cud. Oftentimes the animals are covered in a coating of snow.

During daylight, I spent hours watching the bison push powdery snow aside with their massive heads to reach the dormant grass below. It may take several powerful sweeps of the head to push away enough snow to find a tuft of dried brown grass. My mind races—how can these gargantuan animals survive on such a meager food supply? They spend hours plowing snow just to obtain a small amount of nutrition. How can it be enough to sustain an animal of at least 1,500 pounds? It's amazing that any of the Yellowstone bison can survive. And yet, they seem to thrive.

The elk have a different winter survival tactic. They climb high on the mountainsides, where snow has not accumulated. Sometimes they move to open areas where the wind has blown away the snow, exposing stalks of dried grass. Sure, there may be food at the open locations, but these are also the most unprotected areas with extremely frigid winds.

Bighorn Sheep risk life and limb daily, scrambling onto rocky outcrops with slick patches of ice and snow—just to nibble a bit of dried grass clinging to the rock face. It is at these exposed places where the bighorns find their meager rations of food. Again I watch and photograph for hours and think how difficult life is for these animals. But I also can't imagine a happier existence for them than one that allows them the freedom to live life as they are meant to live it—in the wild. That thought alone keeps me warm on these cold winter days.

Every day I encounter several coyotes trying to eke out a living in this rugged, but beautiful, winter environment. These critters cover many miles each day in search of a meal. They listen for mice and other small rodents under the thick blanket of snow before pouncing. Many times their meals come in the form of hand-me-downs from Yellowstone's top predator, the wolf. After the wolves have killed and eaten their fill, they leave the carcass for the magpies, ravens and coyotes.

But it's not the elk, bighorn, bison or coyote that I have come to photograph. It is the most famous resident of the park—the Gray Wolf (*Canis lupus*). Each night under the cover of darkness, wolves test the other animal residents. If conditions are good and the pack's hunting skill is strong, the wolves will make a kill. If not, they go hungry for another day. This is the life and death drama of Yellowstone.

No animal has the allure and mystique of the Gray Wolf. It's a top predator that represents the ultimate in wilderness and all things wild. It's also an animal near and dear to our hearts because of our close relationship with its first cousin—the domestic dog.

It is mid-February, the height of wolf mating season. The activity of each pack is at a fevered pitch, and each day a new drama unfolds before me. One morning I saw a female wolf in estrus with blood-stained genitals. She was walking around a snowy ridge and stopping every now and then to howl. Eventually she sat and howled for five minutes straight before lying down and falling asleep. Several hours later she woke, stretched and continued her journey to the top of the ridge, where she met and mated with the alpha male of her pack.

During 1995-96, a total of 66 Gray Wolves were reintroduced into Yellowstone after more than 70 years of absence. It was the last piece to complete the park's ecosystems puzzle. They are now flourishing in their place at the top of the food chain.

The main pack I am following has seven members—four females and three males, with four black and three gray. The alpha male, who is black with silver highlights, is busy attending to the alpha female. When the alpha female is lying down or not around, the alpha male is also mating with the subordinate females. Only the alpha female is supposed to breed, so to see this extracurricular activity is very interesting. These animals are not windup toys with a set script of behaviors. They show the unpredictability of nature, and I like that.

The black alpha male is easy to tell apart from the other black wolves in the pack. His yellow eyes shine like two beams of sunlight. He holds his tail high and seems to spend all of his time moving around and visiting with the pack members. He apparently isn't getting much rest or food.

For three days I watch the alpha male spend all of his waking hours chasing after the females in his pack and mate them all. On the fourth day everything changed. A lone gray male wolf that had been loitering for several days in the valley charged into the pack and challenged the residing alpha male. For the next three hours the two fought and chased each other. Finally, the black alpha male was driven off and the new gray male took over as the pack leader. It was stunning to witness. It was not something that had taken place in some distant land and then shown on TV—and the thought of that was also thrilling. It happened right here, right now, in front of me.

The ousted male moved about a half mile away to another ridge. There he climbed to the top, onto a snow-covered rock. Bathed in the last sunlight of the day, he stood and howled across the river valley to his former pack. As the sun set, he began to trot down the side of the ridge straight toward me. I moved forward to get some closer images. He paused at the road nearby, turned to stare at me and then crossed over. Finally, running through the deep snow on the opposite side of the road, he made his way up the hill.

It was obvious where this wolf was heading. Three days ago his pack had killed an elk, and he was heading for the remains. He loped over to see what was left. For the past couple days, magpies, ravens and coyotes had been picking at it, but a meal could still be made. Picking up one of the large hindquarters as if it were a chew toy, the wolf trotted off.

He carried the leg about 300 yards to a large rock in an open field, set it down and looked in all directions before starting to eat. In my mind I could hear what the wolf was thinking. "I need to eat right, exercise regularly and in a couple days I will be going back to fight the new gray male and win my pack back."

It was now dark so I started up the truck and began the long drive back to town. It had been a magnificent day.

Florida Manatee

Florida is a wondrous place filled with a wide variety of plants, animals and birds. For instance, there are nearly 300 species of trees native to Florida and more than 450 species of birds. It's a nature lover's paradise, especially for a northern guy like me in the middle of winter.

Even if you are not a nature nut like me, there is one Florida species that is so unique it captivates even the most citified of people—the Florida Manatee (*Trichechus manatus latirostris*), also called just Manatee or sea cow.

Manatees range from Brazil, Mexico, southeastern United States and the Caribbean islands. The Florida Manatee is one of two subspecies of West Indian Manatee. The other subspecies is the Antillean Manatee, which occurs from Brazil to Mexico. The Florida Manatee is found along the Atlantic Coast from Florida to Georgia and the Carolinas, and also in the Gulf of Mexico from Florida to Texas. However, the main concentration of this endangered species is found in and around Florida.

Manatees are large marine mammals, with adults weighing on average 1,000 pounds, with some as much as 1,500 pounds. They have an average length of 12–14 feet. Like elephants, they continue to grow throughout their lives. The largest manatee ever recorded was 13 feet 4 inches and weighed over 3,200 pounds. You really get the sense of their size when you're swimming with them.

These large aquatic mammals are gray and sparsely covered with hair. They have large forelimbs, which are better described as flippers, and no hind limbs. They do have a large wide tail used for swimming up to 15 miles per hour for short distances. They have tiny eyes, but can see very well, and though they don't have any external ear openings, they do hear very well.

As air-breathing animals, manatees need to surface every 3–5 minutes to breathe, but they can stay submerged for up to 15 minutes if necessary. They are gentle giants, spending most of their day sleeping and feeding on aquatic plants. They consume about 150 pounds of vegetation each day and use their eyesight to find the food.

Female manatees become sexually mature at 4–5 years. Mothers give birth to a single calf once every 2–5 years. Only rarely do they have twins. Calves weigh about 75–90 pounds at birth and are over 6 feet long. Since these are marine mammals, the calves suckle milk from their mothers for the first 5–6 months and start eating aquatic vegetation at 3–5 months.

Manatees appear in the fossil record around 50–60 million years ago. There are many fossilized remains in the American Indian rubbish piles that predate the arrival of the early Spaniards. Today manatees are an endangered species.

Most calves stay with their mothers for up to two years before moving out on their own. During this time the calves learn what kinds of plants are good to eat, where the warm water refuges are located and the migratory route from their mothers.

There are fewer than 3,000 manatees left in the wild. They have no natural enemies except for powerboats (people), which kill many manatees each year. Combine that with a slow reproductive rate and you have a potential for extinction. Because of this, they are listed as an endangered species. If you are ever in their range, it would be well worth your time and effort to see these magnificent marine mammals.

Alaskan Sojourn

I returned from a wonderful Alaskan adventure complete with bone-breaking cold temperatures, snow, erupting volcanoes, avalanches and oceans that never freeze. Alaska is the real deal when it comes to wildlife and wild places, and I'm never disappointed when I go there. Nowhere else can you find such an abundance of birds and mammals on both land and sea.

It may seem crazy to visit our largest state during winter, but I think it's a magical season. The snow-covered mountains and winter landscapes help make it a beautiful time to be in the Land of the Midnight Sun, even though the days are incredibly short. I spent most of my visit along the coast of the Kenai Peninsula. This stretch of land juts southwest out of Anchorage and is surrounded by Kachemak Bay.

Driving through the mountains that dominate the scenery, I saw more moose in 10 days than I had over several years of other travel. The streams there flow with icy green water the consistency of a slurpy. At first glance, the slush looks uninhabitable, but swimming in the ice water are Common Goldeneyes and Barrow's Goldeneyes. These stunning black and white ducks dive quickly beneath the rushing ice to catch aquatic insects and crustaceans along the river bottom.

Along Alaska's riverbanks lives·the American Dipper—a small gray bird that looks like an American Robin or Gray Catbird. The Dipper is another cold-tolerant bird. With much zest and gusto, it dives headfirst into fast-moving streams that would sweep you or me away to our deaths in seconds. Under the surface, it captures tiny aquatic insects and brings them up to eat at the water's edge. Afterward, it turns and dives into the freezing water again for a repeat fishing trip. What an amazing tiny bird!

One of my all-time favorite animals is the Sea Otter. You can see these playful critters nearly anywhere on the coast. Once when I stopped to photograph a huge flock of Rock Sandpipers, I saw about 300 otters swimming, loafing in the water and floating on icebergs. I've seen large groups of otters in southern California, but never this big. I watched as some would roll around on their backs, enjoying the sunshine and feeding on clams and other shellfish, while others would play-fight. Such delight!

This was also my first experience with an active volcano. Just a couple weeks before my trip, Mount Augustine erupted and now I was driving right past it. I can tell you that I kept my eye on that smoking plume! Thankfully, it didn't erupt again during my stay. Just seeing the volcano active only 75 miles away was thrilling enough.

The weather alternated between days of snow and sunshine. Air temps seemed to be no more than 30 degrees during the day. Nights were in the single digits until the last two days, when temps dropped like a rock. One day while photographing Boreal Chickadees (similar to our Black-capped Chickadees), the temperature was at best 20 degrees below zero. Coming from Minnesota I was well prepared for extreme conditions, but that kind of weather can make you feel really alive!

I traveled Alaska mainly to photograph Bald Eagles. The town of Homer is the winter home to several hundred of these magnificent birds. I spent many days photographing eagles fishing in the ocean, resting on rocky beaches, and soaring and banking with snowy peaks as a backdrop. I took thousands of images of these raptors, documenting their behaviors and natural history. Even after a week of photographing, it was still exciting to rise each morning before daybreak to photograph these great birds. Many of these images are shown in *Majestic Eagles: Compelling Facts and Images of the Bald Eagle*, a nature appreciation book I wrote to celebrate our national symbol.

Druid Wolf Encounters

Thick clouds laden with snow cling to the mountaintops surrounding the wide valley before me. Fortunately, the wind is dead calm, because the air temperatures are 15–18 degrees below zero. In the distance I can hear the low mournful howl of a lone wolf. It is a true and absolute sound of nature that I never get tired of hearing.

I'm back from my annual winter trip to Yellowstone National Park. This magnificent park has an intact ecosystem complete with the top predator, the Gray Wolf (*Canis lupus*). On this trip, two photographers from around the country joined me to find and photograph wolves.

I think many people who have not had any experience with wolves may have some faulty ideas about these close relatives of our family dogs. Wolves are not bloodthirsty killers that run around the countryside killing indiscriminately, just for the fun of it. I can tell you that in all my years of studying and photographing wolves, I have never seen anything even remotely approaching this kind of behavior. In fact, it's just the opposite.

Our first encounter with a wolf occurred within a day of our arrival. It was a large, heavily battle-scarred gray female, but the event was most notable because she was alone. She was moving across the mountains and valleys in search of a mate or a pack that would accept her. For several days she had been trying to work her way into the famed Druid pack—a well-known pack that controls a large territory in Yellowstone. According to the park's wolf biologist, this female had been successful at taking down a female elk entirely by herself and she was allowing the Druid pack to feed on her kill. It was a gesture of goodwill, but the established Druid female leaders still would not allow the lone female into the pack.

The next day the neighboring Black-tailed pack made a kill near the Druid's territory, and the Druids ventured over for something to eat. They hadn't eaten in many days, and many were suffering from mange, a disease of intense itching and hair loss that is caused by a parasitic mite. It was obvious that this pack was not doing well. Predictably, the Black-tailed pack successfully defended their food by attacking the Druid intruders, and a savage fight broke out. The Druid alpha female was severely injured, with several large lacerations in her neck.

The Druids retreated to their territory only to find the lone gray female waiting for them. Taking out their frustration on her, the pack attacked and drove her off. The lone female limped away from the encounter, but otherwise seemed okay.

After the attack, we watched the Druid pack lick their wounds. It was sad. The wolves were starving to death, about half of the members had mange and it was clear that they were in bad shape. The severely injured alpha female was not doing well at all. She just stood there, head down and wavering from side to side. It was sunset and the temperatures were dropping, so we packed up with a sense of foreboding.

The following morning we returned to the valley at first light only to find that our fears had come true. The badly wounded alpha female was dead. Her frozen, lifeless body lay still in the snow. The park biologist retrieved her body and brought it back to the road, where we all got a close look at the pain and misery that wolves face every day.

But where were the rest of the Druid pack? And where was the lone gray female that was so desperately seeking to gain acceptance?

We drove east, up and through the narrow rocky pass. On the other side is the Lamar Valley. The valley is wide with a shallow river meandering through the center. Scanning the mountainsides along the way, we were unsuccessful at locating any wildlife. It was still early in the day, and the clouds were thick and heavy with snow. About 3–4 miles into the valley on the north side, we were surprised to locate the lone gray female. She was sitting with the two black male wolves from the Druid pack.

Now this was interesting! The gray female was a good 10 miles east of where we saw her previously, but what was more amazing was that two very healthy male wolves accompanied her. The three stood up, shaking off the snow that had begun to fall. They greeted each other with face licks and wagging tails, a normal behavior for all canids and a good sign that they were forming their own pack. We were thrilled to see this! They appeared to be happy together, and we talked about the possibility of a new pack forming right before our eyes. Then the three turned and walked up the mountain to the ridge, where they disappeared out of sight.

At the end of the day, about 30 minutes before the sun slipped behind the mountains west of the Lamar Valley, an extraordinary event unfolded before us. While photographing a coyote near the road, we suddenly noticed elk running through the snow on top of the mountain ridge in front of us. We swung our cameras up to get a better look and saw a herd of about 20 females racing across the snowy ridge. Following in hot pursuit was the gray female wolf followed by the two black males. The hunt was on!

The elk and the wolves both ran behind the ridge. Predicting that they would emerge a bit to the east, we piled into my truck and headed in that direction. As expected, a lone female elk appeared on the ridge running hard and fast, apparently with a wolf close on her tail. A second later the gray female wolf appeared on the same ridge, running in deep snow. The elk turned and started to race down the mountain right toward us.

We pulled into a parking lot with a small group of buildings to get a better vantage point. We could see the gray wolf making huge leaps through the deep snow as she ran down the mountainside. She was about 75 feet behind the elk, which made her too far back to get a picture of both the elk and wolf together.

Passing behind the buildings the elk made a break for the road. Again we piled back into my truck and pulled out onto the road and stopped. About 300 yards in front of us the elk crossed the road at a full run. We could clearly see that she was out of breath and struggling to keep going. Next, the wolf hit the deep snowbanks lining the road and did a face-plant, stopping her in her tracks, but she but managed to recover and continue the pursuit. However, she had lost valuable ground. The elk ran out across the valley heading directly for the river. We all knew what this meant. The elk was heading for the safety of the river, knowing the wolf wouldn't enter the deeper freezing water where the elk's long legs would allow her to stand.

The elk made it to the river, and from a great distance we could see the water splashing as she ran into the deep part. Moments later the wolf arrived and then abruptly stopped pursuit. It was a standoff. Now we would see just how determined the female wolf would be. Would she wait out the elk or give up and return?

Meanwhile, behind us the two black male wolves appeared on the ridge looking for the female. They started howling, but got no response. About 30 minutes later the female howled faintly. Apparently she had given up the standoff and was trotting across the valley toward the males. Upon meeting, the males mobbed her and greeted her with many licks and wagging tails. The three looked so happy to be with one another.

By now the light was gone and darkness surrounded us. The three wolves loped up the mountain into the shadows, still hungry, but in the comfort of each other. A new pack was formed.

Index

About the Author

Naturalist, wildlife photographer and writer Stan Tekiela is the originator of the popular state-specific field guide series that includes *Birds of Arkansas Field Guide*. For over two decades, Stan has authored more than 100 field guides, nature appreciation books and wildlife audio CDs for nearly every state in the nation, presenting many species of birds, mammals, reptiles and amphibians, trees, wildflowers and cacti.

Holding a Bachelor of Science degree in Natural History from the University of Minnesota and as an active professional naturalist for more than 20 years, Stan studies and photographs wildlife throughout the United States and has received various national and regional awards for his books and photographs. Also a well-known columnist and radio personality, his syndicated column appears in over 20 newspapers and his wildlife programs are broadcast on a number of Midwest radio stations. He is a member of the North American Nature Photography Association and Canon Professional Services. Stan resides in Victoria, Minnesota, with his wife, Katherine, and daughter, Abigail. He can be contacted via his web page at www.naturesmart.com.